You're in **1**

Your c........ are being hurt **23**

Your children are missing **47**

You're angry or depressed **77**

Your money is gone **101**

State information **129**

Divorce First Aid

Protect Yourself From Domestic Violence, Parental Kidnapping, Property Theft, and Other Divorce Emergencies

Webster Watnik

Cover design and illustration by Lightbourne Images copyright © 2001.

Library of Congress Catalog Card Number: 97-62193

Publisher's Cataloging in Publication

Watnik, Webster.
   Divorce first aid: protect yourself from domestic violence, parental kidnapping, property theft, and other divorce emergencies / Webster Watnik.
   p. cm.
   Includes appendix.
   ISBN: 0-9649404-1-8

1. Divorce. 2. Divorced people—Crimes against. 3. Divorced people—Crimes against—Prevention. Domestic relations. 5. Family violence. I. Title

HQ814.W38   2001
306.89   QBI97-41443

Single Parent Press
P.O. Box 1298
Claremont, CA 91711
(909) 624-6058 phone
(909) 624-2208 fax

Thank you to the beautiful Alicia for reading and to the wonderful Shannon for great art work. Also, thanks to my buddy, Michael.

This book is dedicated to Wyeth.

Table of contents

You're angry or depressed 77

Your money is gone 101

State information 129

You're in danger

You're in an abusive relationship

Many couples have problems, but sometimes the problems go too far. When behavior crosses the line into abuse, you have to recognize it and deal with it.

Recognize the symptoms

If you can answer "yes" to any of the following questions, then you're in an abusive relationship.

- Does your spouse hit you?
- Does your spouse threaten you?
- Does your spouse constantly criticize you?
- Does your spouse throw or break objects?
- Does your spouse control all the money?
- Is your spouse so jealous that you cannot see your family or friends?
- Does your spouse hurt or threaten the children?

An abuser uses threats or violence to control you. Abuse isn't just being hit. If your spouse has cut you off from your family or friends—that's abuse. Or if your spouse controls all the money leaving you completely helpless—that's abuse.

Abuse affects everyone

Abuse is known by many names—*domestic violence, family violence,* and *spouse abuse.* Abuse cuts across all races and economic lines. It doesn't matter how much money you have, or where you live, or what religion you are. If your spouse is controlling you through threats and violence, you are in an abusive relationship.

The abuse cycle

Abusive relationships often follow a predictable pattern.

First, there is a gradual building of tension. Many people describe this phase as "walking on eggs." The abuser grows angrier. The victim becomes more submissive.

Then it erupts. The violence may last a few moments or a few days. It may even be interrupted when the abuser leaves the house and then returns.

Afterwards, it's calm. During this "honeymoon" phase, the abuser is sorry and swears it will never happen again.

Then the cycle is repeated. But over time, it gets worse.

Why you stay

There are a lot of reasons why you might stay in an abusive relationship.

Maybe you're too ashamed to admit you're being abused. Or you're too scared to leave. Or you don't have enough money. Or you think that if you do leave, your spouse will become even more violent towards you.

And you may be right. If you leave, your spouse may find you and hurt you. Or you may be reduced to poverty. These are problems you will have to deal with.

Go to counseling

Sometimes, you can change an abusive relationship. It's difficult, but not impossible.

One option is to go to counseling or therapy. If your spouse doesn't want to go, you can go by yourself. You can discuss the problems and your options with the counselor.

Seeing a counselor may help, or it may not. It all depends on whether your spouse is willing to change. The Program Director for Emerge, a battering prevention program, estimated that 25% of people in the program succeed.

You will know if counseling is effective if your spouse accepts responsibility for his behavior and he's willing to go to counseling on his own.

If counseling does not work and the abuse continues, then you have to protect yourself.

66 Many women have said that, in retrospect, once their husbands discovered they could get away with being violent, it seemed to lower their inhibitions against future and more severe abuse. *Dr. Kathleen H. Hofeller, Battered Women, Shattered Lives* 99

4

You need to create a safety plan

If you need to leave home because of abuse, prepare by creating a safety plan. A safety plan, or exit plan, contains the information you need and a checklist of things to take if you have to leave home quickly.

Here's a brief safety plan. Review it and add more information, if necessary.

Telephone numbers

Babysitter   _____

Bank   _____

Daycare   _____

District Attorney   _____

Doctor   _____

Emergency Shelter   _____

Family Member   _____

Friend   _____

Hospital   _____

Lawyer   _____

Neighbor   _____

Pastor   _____

Police   _____

Relative   _____

School   _____

Work   _____

Safety Measures

At home, I will protect myself by:
- Staying away from the kitchen—where my spouse can find weapons.
- Staying away from the bathroom, closets, or other small spaces—where my spouse can trap me.
- Going to a room with a door or window to escape.
- Keeping a phone in a room I can lock from the inside.
- Planning an escape route out of my home.
- Packing a bag with money, an extra set of keys, and important documents, and leaving it with a family member or friend.
- Finding a shelter where I can go in an emergency.

I will protect my children by:
- Telling them not to get into the middle of a fight.
- Telling them not to go into the kitchen during a fight.
- Teaching them to call 911.
- Giving the school a copy of the court order.
- Asking the school or daycare not to give out my address to anyone.

At work, I will protect myself by:
- Driving a different route to work.
- Getting rides with different people.
- Telling my supervisor.
- Giving a copy of my court order and a photograph of my spouse to the Security Officer.
- Screening my phone calls.

I will also protect myself by:
- Opening a private mailbox.
- Opening my own bank account.

Papers to take

When I leave, I will take the following papers:
- Driver's license and registration
- Birth certificate
- Social security card
- Passport
- Money
- Checkbook and ATM card
- Credit cards
- House deed, mortgage payment book
- Income tax statements
- Medical records
- Protection order
- Divorce papers
- Address book
- Safety plan
- Children's birth certificates
- Children's social security cards
- Children's school records
- Children's medical records

Items to take

When I leave, I will take the following items:
- Keys to the house and car
- Pictures and jewelry
- Objects of sentimental value
- Clothes
- Medications
- Children's clothes
- Children's toys
- Children's medications

You need to call the police

If you are being hurt and can get to a phone safely, call the police.

Call 911

When the police arrive, they must find out what happened. They will talk to you and your spouse.

When it is your turn, tell the police what happened. If you have any evidence such as a black eye, bruises, or wounds—show the police.

Often, the police will make an official report. If they don't make a report—ask them to.

After finding out what happened, the police may decide to arrest your spouse. Or they may offer to take you and your children to a shelter. Or they may offer to help you get a protective order.

If the police do not arrest your spouse and you are still afraid, ask them to escort you out.

Arresting your spouse

It is against the law for your spouse to hurt you. But in many places, the police do not have to arrest your spouse—it is up to their discretion.

8

If you want the police to arrest your spouse, show them evidence your spouse has committed a crime. You can convince the police by showing them bruises or injuries.

If your spouse is arrested, you are not safe. It may only take a few hours for your spouse to be released, and he may return home. If you are afraid that will happen, use the time while he is gone to leave your home.

The attitude of the police

Police feel that coming to your home is volatile and unpredictable. They may not arrest your spouse because they think you will change your mind, or if the District Attorney does prosecute your spouse, you will not cooperate. You must convince the police that you want the abuse to stop.

Should you fight back?

If you fight back, you may win—but you may not. If you try to hurt your spouse but only wound him, he could turn around and kill you. Or if you do kill your spouse, you may be charged with a crime and go to jail.

66 From my own experiences as a police officer I have seen family members who have been shot, stabbed, slugged, slapped, had bones broken, had scalding liquids thrown on them, been run over by cars, run over by lawn mowers, hit with bats, shovels and rakes, beaten with an electrical cord, assaulted with chain saws, and thrown from moving cars.
Captain Robert L. Snow, Family Abuse 99

You need a restraining order

When your spouse threatens to hurt you or your children, a court can order your spouse to stay away. This is called a *protective order, restraining order,* or *peace bond.*

What a restraining order does

A restraining order tells your spouse to stay away from you. It may also tell your spouse to stay away from your home, your work, to not follow you or call you, and to stay away from the children. It may also prevent your spouse from taking any money out of your joint checking account.

If your spouse ignores a restraining order, he can be arrested.

How to get a restraining order

1. Go to court. If you don't know where the courthouse is, ask the police.

2. At court, ask an official where you get papers for a restraining order.

3. Fill out the papers. Explain why you want the restraining order. If the police have been to your home, get a copy of the police report. If you have photographs of bruises or other evidence of being hurt, bring them to court.

4. Go to the hearing. After you fill out the papers, you will talk to a Judge. Sometimes you can do it the same day, sometimes you have to wait until the next day.

In some communities, you may be able to talk to the Judge without your spouse. In other places, you have to tell your spouse you are taking him to court.

No matter what happens, the restraining orders will only last a few days, and then you will have to go back to court to tell the Judge why you want the orders to become permanent.

Serving the order

Once you get a restraining order, give a copy to the police. If something happens, the police will be able to act faster.

You also have to give your spouse a copy. The police may do it, or you can find people who will give the restraining order to your spouse by looking in the phone book for the *marshal* or a *process server.*

When court is closed

If court is closed, the police can create an emergency order that tells your spouse to stay away. This will only last a short time, and if you want the order to last, you will have to go to court when it opens and ask for a permanent order.

Taking precautions

A piece of paper will not protect you if your spouse wants to hurt you. That's why some people believe "a restraining order is a way of getting killed faster." In addition to getting an order, you should do other things to protect yourself. Look around your home to see where you are vulnerable. If your spouse has a set of keys—change the locks. If your doors are made of thin wood—get stronger doors installed, or at least thicker jambs.

When it's time to take the children to school, alternate your routes. The same holds true for going to work—alternate the roads you drive, and don't go to the same place for lunch.

If you feel you are still in danger, you will have to leave your home and move to a secure place.

66 While protection orders are a valuable tool for dealing with domestic violence issues, they are routinely abused. Parents trying to prevail in custody disputes commonly manipulate the court system by offering false affidavits in order to obtain an emergency, ex parte order (one-party testimony) giving them custody. These and other ex parte orders are plentiful, and it is not unusual for each parent to brandish conflicting orders obtained from different local courts. *Missing and Abducted Children: A Law Enforcement Guide to Case Investigation and Program Management* 99

You need emergency shelter

Sometimes violence escalates to the point where you must leave. If you are afraid for your safety, do not wait. Call a hotline and ask for help. Find out where you can go in an emergency—then go there.

Call a hotline

Look in the front of your phone book. You may find a phone number for a local crises hotline. If you can't find a local number, call this number:

800-799-7233

This is the *National Domestic Violence Hotline.* It is staffed 24 hours-a-day. The people who answer the phone can refer you to local resources in the continental United States, Puerto Rico, Hawaii, and Alaska. By calling a hotline, you can find out how to protect yourself and where you can go for help.

Seek shelter

There are thousands of emergency shelters available. If you are in danger and you must leave your home, go to an emergency shelter. To find a shelter, call:

911

If the police do not help you, you can also call: a hospital, a church, a newspaper, the court, or a woman's organization.

Protect yourself

If you are going to leave—be careful! Leaving is a dangerous time. If you tell your spouse you're leaving, he may get angry. The two most dangerous times are when you decide to leave and when you start a new relationship.

Once you reach the shelter, you'll be safe. The location of the emergency shelter is kept secret. Your spouse will not find out where you are.

The shelter will provide you with food and a place to sleep. You will still need to find work and a permanent place to live. The shelter may have people who can help you, including a counselor, a doctor, and a lawyer.

Protect your children

If you have children and you want to take them with you, be aware that some shelters do not accept children. Check first.

Also, try and get court orders allowing you to take the children with you—otherwise you may be kidnapping them. You can get emergency orders from the court. The police also have the authority to protect the children.

If you leave without permission to take the children, immediately notify the police where the children are, and that you had a reason to fear for the children's safety. That is not kidnapping.

Don't let family and friends discourage you. "Outsiders" may not want to take sides. Or they may have other reasons why they don't want to help.

To walk away from your spouse, you must be able to be alone, and you must be ready to take personal responsibility. To leave, you must say "goodbye" to the marriage.

66 Most women, wanting to make the relationship work, will try to figure out rationally how they can change their own behavior to help the batterer stop battering... But because the abuser intends a coercion far more profound than any immediate 'reason' for any particular incident, whatever the woman does—short of surrendering utterly to his will—must fail. *Ann Jones, Next Time, She'll Be Dead* 99

You want to file charges

If you've been abused, you may be able to "press charges" against your spouse.

Pressing charges means the District Attorney accuses your spouse of committing a crime—such as battery. Battery is a serious crime, and if your spouse is found guilty, he may be seriously punished.

How to file charges

To file charges, you must go to the police station and sign a *complaint.* In your complaint, you describe how you were abused. The complaint is then sent to the District Attorney or local prosecutor.

After reading your complaint, the prosecutor decides whether to file charges or not. If the prosecutor believes he can prove your spouse abused you, he will file charges. In some communities, the prosecutor must automatically file charges once your complaint is made.

Misdemeanor vs. felony

Depending on the laws in your state, your spouse may be charged with either a misdemeanor or a felony.

A misdemeanor is a minor crime, and carries a smaller punishment—such as a maximum of one year in jail and a

16

$1,000 fine. A felony is a major crime, and your spouse can be punished by spending many, many years in jail.

Types of evidence

To prove you were abused, your statements are very important, but you may also need other evidence, including:
- Photographs or videotapes showing an assault or bruises.
- A diary with dates, times, and a description of the abuse.
- The testimony of a psychologist or a doctor.
- A tape recording (if your state allows secret recordings).
- Police reports of the abuse.
- Previous criminal arrests and convictions of your spouse.

Sue your spouse

You may be able to sue your spouse for what he did to you. All states have laws that let you recover money from someone who has hurt you. However, many states specifically prevent married people from suing each other.

If you want to sue your spouse, ask a lawyer to see if your state allows you to sue.

66 Any misconduct on your husband's part can be abuse. If your husband battered, tormented, or assaulted you, these are all considered examples of abuse. If he told you that you are fat, ignorant, or from a low-class family, these statements are also abusive. *Bradley A. Pistotnik, Divorce War!* 99

You've been kicked out

If your spouse has accused you of abusing her, you may have been "kicked out" of your home.

If you are fighting and the police come to your home, they may tell you to leave. Or a judge may order you to move out. Or your spouse may simply lock you out.

What to do

If you are kicked out and the police have not been contacted, call them to see if there is a restraining order. If there is no order, contact a lawyer and insist on going to court. You can ask a Judge to let you return to your home.

For many reasons, you may not be allowed back into your home. However, you can ask the police or a sheriff to accompany you for a brief time to pick up your clothes and other things.

What not to do

If you've been kicked out, do not "take the law into your own hands." Do not break down a door or sneak back in through a window.

If the police ordered you to leave and you return, you will be arrested and charged with a crime. If a Judge ordered you to stay away and you ignore the order, you can be put in jail and charged with contempt of court.

The effect on custody

Being kicked out of your home will have an effect on custody of your children. That's because when the Judge decides custody, he wants to keep the living arrangements for the children the same.

If your children stay in the home but you leave, you will have to be allowed back into your home, or else convince the Judge that you should remove the children. Both are difficult.

The bias against men

Police officers and judges often treat men more harshly than women. Yes, a woman can assault a man just as easily as a man can assault a woman. However, when police officers come to your home and try to figure out what happened, it is possible that your spouse will be believed even though she is lying.

Bias is a fact of life, and you will have to deal with it.

66 Everyone knows that restraining orders and orders to vacate are granted to virtually all who apply. It has become impossible to effectively represent a man against whom any allegation of domestic violence has been made. In virtually all cases, no notice, meaningful hearing, or impartial weighing of evidence is to be had. The courts frequently seem to have taken a rubber stamp approach to dispensing of such orders. *Elaine Epstein, former president of the Massachusetts Bar Association* 99

Where to get help

National Domestic Violence Hotline
800-799-7233
This number is staffed 24 hours-a-day. Call for help or for a referral to an emergency shelter.

National Coalition Against Domestic Violence
www.ncadv.org
This web site has referrals to an attorney in your area. See "Getting Help."

Rape, Abuse, & Incest National Network (RAINN)
800-656-4673
www.rainn.org
Call for free counseling or to locate a crisis center. See "Counseling Centers."

Department of Justice, Violence Against Women Office
www.ojp.usdoj.gov/vawo
Contains a list of state hotlines. See "Help and Information Near You."

NOW Legal Defense and Education Fund
www.nowldef.org
The web site for the National Organization for Women. See "Publications and Resources."

More reading

There are many books on domestic abuse. New books are published all the time, and old books go out-of-print. Here are some sample titles:

Breaking Free from Partner Abuse: Voices of Battered Women Caught in the Cycle of Domestic Violence, Mary Marecek, Jami Moffett (Illustrator), Jeanne W. Lindsay, Jamie Moffett, Morning Glory Press, 1999. Mixing poetry and prose, this sensitive book is for women who are experiencing violence in a relationship.

Defending Our Lives: Getting Away from Domestic Violence and Staying Safe, Susan Murphy-Milano, 1996. This book offers practical, step-by-step advice to battered women on protecting themselves.

Family Abuse: Tough Solutions to Stop the Violence, Robert L. Snow, Plenum Press, 1997. Based on a lifetime of police work, Captain Snow offers stunning eyewitness descriptions of family violence.

Getting Free: You Can End Abuse and Take Back Your Life, Ginny Nicarthy, 1997. The bible of all domestic violence texts. This book describes the problems—and solutions—to domestic violence through the voices of women who share their experiences.

Next Time, She'll Be Dead: Battering and How to Stop It, Ann Jones, Beacon Press, 1994. A compelling book about spouse abuse. A classic.

Surviving Domestic Violence: Voices of Women Who Broke Free, Elaine Weiss, Agreka Books, 2000. This well-written book contains interviews with domestic violence survivors.

When Love Goes Wrong: What to Do When You Can't Do Anything Right, Ann Jones, Susan Schechter, 1993. This book provides guidance and practical options for women in controlling and abusive relationships.

When Men Batter Women: New Insights into Ending Abusive Relationships, Neil S., Ph.D. Jacobson, John Mordechai Gottman, Simon and Schuster, 1998. Based on a decade of research with more than 200 couples, the authors shed new light on abusive relationships.

Your children are being hurt

23

You lose control when you discipline your children

Parenting is not easy. You love your children and want them to be happy. But sometimes, your children misbehave. And when that happens—you have to discipline them.

When disciplining your children, it's easy to become frustrated or angry. All parents get angry at times. But you have to remain in control and not hurt your children.

Five ways to keep control when you discipline your children

1. Take a deep breath. Then another one. By focusing on your breathing, you can force yourself to calm down.

2. Phone a friend. When you call someone, you can blow off steam and not direct it at your children.

3. Take a bath or a shower. Arrange for the children to be watched by someone, then take a long, hot bath.

4. Turn on some music and sing along. Cheerful music will divert you from the anger of the moment.

5. Grab a pillow. You can punch it, lay your head down on it—anything. Pillows are very handy.

24

Don't spank

Spanking your child seems simple, fast, and effective. If your child is misbehaving—wham! A quick slap will straighten him out.

But almost all child care experts agree that spanking is wrong. If you spank, you do not teach your child how to behave correctly. You only teach your child how to avoid being hit again. There is a huge difference. And when you spank, you also run the risk of hurting your child. Then you are abusing him.

You can teach your children how to behave with other techniques.

Effective ways to discipline

If you feel the pressure building and you think you will hit your child, try one of these alternatives.

Put your child in "time out." You can tell your child to sit quietly in a chair. The rule is one minute for every year of the child's age.

Take away privileges. You can take away TV or toys or playing with a friend. This tactic works best when you want to correct a specific misbehavior.

Assign work detail. Older children can do jobs around the house—such as washing the car or taking out the garbage. Even younger children can help with the dishes.

Redirect behavior. If your child is throwing things, hand him a ball. If he wrote on the wall, give him a piece of paper.

Set the example. Children do as you do, not as you say. If you want your children to obey the rules—you have to obey the rules.

Take care of yourself

When you discipline your children, you're also dealing with your own feelings. Maybe your child's behavior reminds you of something that happened when you were a child. Or maybe you're angry about something else. Or maybe you feel alone and taken for granted.

Stop and think about what is bothering you, and how you can resolve it. You may find that your children are not the problem—it's something else. After you separate your problems from the children, it will be easier to control the kids.

❝ It is difficult to imagine that any person would intentionally inflict harm on his or her own child. Many times physical abuse is a result of excessive over-discipline or physical punishment that is inappropriate for the child's age. The parent may simply be unaware of the magnitude of force with which he or she strikes a child. Most parents want to be good parents, but sometimes they lose control and are unable to cope. *American Humane Society* ❞

You suspect your children are being abused

Most people take good care of their children... but some do not. If you think your child is being hurt, you must find out.

What is child abuse?

Child abuse is hurting a child. If a child is battered or molested—that's child abuse. If a parent ignores a child's needs—that neglect is also abuse.

There are four categories of child abuse:

Physical Abuse. This is when a child is physically injured. Slapping, kicking, hitting, burning—all are examples of physical abuse. With an infant, "Shaken Baby Syndrome"— where a baby is shaken so violently that his brain slams into his skull—is physical abuse.

Sexual Abuse. When a child is involved in a sexual activity it is sexual abuse. It includes everything from showing a child pornography to having intercourse with the child. Fondling, masturbating and indecent exposure are all examples of sexual child abuse.

Emotional Abuse. Humiliating a child, constantly criticizing a child, severely shaming a child—these are examples of emotional abuse. Children need positive encouragement, and terrorizing or constantly rejecting a child is abuse.

Neglect. Child neglect is ignoring a child's basic needs. If a child is severely underfed, is never brought to a doctor, or is left alone for long periods of time—that is child neglect. Neglect is the long-term pattern of failing to take good care of a child.

Recognize the symptoms

If a child is being abused, there may be some external signs. If he is being physically hurt, he will have bruises or broken bones. If he is being neglected, he may have poor hygiene or miss a lot of school.

But children rarely admit when they are being abused. To find out if your child is being hurt, you may have to look for other symptoms, such as:
- Bed-wetting, nightmares, or fear of going to bed.
- Depression or self-neglect.
- Acting out abuse with a toy.
- Tattered or filthy clothing.
- Refusal to take part in gym class.
- Sophisticated sexual knowledge.

Talk to a doctor or therapist

During divorce, it is common for one parent to falsely accuse the other of child abuse. For that reason, abuse accusations are not always believed.

If you think your child is being hurt, talk to your child's doctor or to a therapist. You can find a therapist who handles abuse cases by calling the local child abuse hotline or by asking the police for a list of rape or crisis centers. The therapist will want to know exactly what you think happened. You must feel comfortable with the therapist and honestly describe the problem.

If the therapist agrees that your child is being harmed, you can ask him to come to court and testify before the Judge.

Religious beliefs

Some parents are members of a religion that restricts conventional medical care. If your religion limits the medical care that your child receives, you must not physically harm your child, or it is child abuse.

66 When a child discloses physical or sexual abuse or behavior in a way that makes you believe there has been abuse, it is natural for a parent to question the child to try to learn more about what may have happened. You should be aware, however, that law enforcement and the courts sometimes view this questioning as contaminating the child's statement. Thus, you must proceed carefully in order to avoid being accused of coaching the child. For instance, be careful to keep your questioning minimal; do not interrogate and re-interrogate your child. Take her to a medical professional to be examined, but be aware that...a physical examination may not reveal everything that is happening to your child because some forms of sexual abuse, such as fondling, do not leave physical evidence. *National Organization of Women* 99

You must report child abuse

If a child is being hurt, you must report it. You can make a report by telling many people, including teachers, the police, or a child abuse hotline.

Call a hotline

To make a report, look in the front of your phone book for the child abuse hotline. If you can't find a local number, call:

800-422-4453

This is the *ChildHelp USA National Child Abuse Hotline.* It is staffed 24 hours-a-day. The people who answer will help you decide if your child is being abused and how you can report the abuse to a child protective agency in your area.

In addition to the child abuse hotline, you can also call your local police, or you can tell your child's doctor, teacher, nurse, or daycare worker.

Tell a mandated reporter

The law requires many people to report child abuse. That includes just about everyone who has contact with a child—doctors, nurses, psychologists, social workers, teachers, and day care workers.

If you tell one of these *mandated reporters* your child is being hurt, she will make an official report. In fact, most child abuse reports come from mandated reporters.

Make the report

When you report child abuse, you will be asked some questions, including your name, the child's name, your relationship with the child, and your reasons for suspecting abuse.

When you make a report, you don't have to say your name. However, if you make an anonymous report, it will be more difficult for the investigator to decide if the report is real.

" The law compels a wide range of people who have contact with children to report suspected child abuse or neglect. A person who is required to report suspected neglect or abuse may face civil or criminal penalties for failure to do so. In addition, states often encourage the reporting of suspected abuse by others such as neighbors and family members through special hot lines. The laws of most states encourage persons to make reports of abuse by granting them immunity from defamation suits by the accused parents if they make the report in good faith. *National Clearinghouse on Child Abuse and Neglect Information* "

A child abuse complaint is being investigated

Once a child abuse complaint is made, a police officer or social worker will investigate.

To find out what happened, the investigator may come into your home, talk to your child, talk to you and your spouse, and physically examine your child.

Interview the children

When talking to your child, the police officer or social worker will ask open-ended questions that do not "plant" ideas into your child's imagination.

Questions such as "Can you tell me what happened?" or "I see you're upset, would you like to talk about it?" are standard interview questions when investigating abuse.

Your child will answer in his own words, and the investigator will evaluate his statements for *indicators* of abuse.

Interview the parents

The investigator may also talk to you and your spouse. If your child is physically hurt, the investigator may ask for an explanation. When evaluating your responses, the investigator will compare your answers with the information given by your child.

Examine the child

Finally, the investigator may physically examine your child. Children who have been physically abused may have burns or bruises. Children who have been sexually abused may have semen or pubic hair on their genitals or clothes. Neglected children may be severely undernourished.

Sometimes the investigator may take your child to the hospital. If there is evidence of abuse, the investigator wants to preserve it. Or, if the investigator believes your child has been hurt before, he may want to x-ray your child for old injuries.

Cooperate with the investigation

You will be asked to cooperate with the investigation. Do it. However, because child abuse is very serious, you should talk to a lawyer before talking to the investigator. If you have to go to court, having a lawyer will help protect your rights.

❝ Unless there is a specific reason for disbelieving or questioning a child's statements, a child's otherwise credible statements should not be discounted or disregarded. *Child Abuse: A Police Guide* ❞

A child abuse complaint was "indicated" or "substantiated"

After a police officer or social worker investigates a child abuse complaint, she will decide if the report is genuine.

If the investigator decides your child was not abused, she will say the report is "unfounded" and the investigation is over. But if the investigator decides your child was abused, she will say the abuse is "indicated" or "substantiated."

Home services

If the investigator believes your child is not in immediate danger and the abuse can be stopped, your child will be left with you. Since most complaints of child abuse do not involve immediate harm to the child—children are often left with their parents.

When deciding whether to leave a child, the investigator will look for a support system of family and friends who can help raise the child. The investigator will also look to see if the adult who hurt the child accepts responsibility for his actions and is willing to change.

If your child is left with you, a social worker will then discuss how to fix the problems that led to the abuse.

There are many solutions to stopping abuse, including programs and parenting classes offered privately and through the courts. You will be told about these programs and given a chance to participate.

If you follow the recommendations made by the social worker, your child will stay with you, and the social worker will return periodically to check up on you.

Eventually, if there are no more problems, the social worker will "close" your file and the services will end.

66 Doctors at hospital emergency rooms find many abusing parents will bring a child in claiming the child has hurt him- or herself 'in a fall' or 'while playing.' However, there is often evidence of repeated violence in the child's medical record, healed broken bones, or extensive bruising in places other than where the child was injured 'accidentally.'
Captain Robert L. Snow, Family Abuse 99

Your children were taken from you

If the police officer or social worker who investigates an abuse complaint decides your child is in immediate danger, she will take the child from your home.

In some states, only a police officer can place a child into *protective custody.* In other states, a social worker can also do it.

Even if the social worker cannot immediately take your child, she can ask the court for an *emergency summons* allowing the child to be removed. These requests are routinely granted.

Protective custody

There are many kinds of abuse that justify taking a child. Some examples include:
- The child was beaten or burned.
- The child was tortured or severely punished.
- The child was severely neglected.
- The home is too dangerous for the child to stay in.
- The parents do not understand the child is being hurt.
- The child was sexually abused.

If the police officer or social worker is convinced your child is in immediate danger, she will often ask you to let your child be removed from your home. Some parents—feeling overwhelmed by the demands of child-rearing—voluntarily give up their child.

But if you do not agree and the investigator believes your child is in danger, she will remove your child anyway.

When your child is removed, he will be taken to an emergency shelter, the home of a relative, a foster home, or a group home. And he will not return until you have had a court hearing.

Emergency hearing

Once a child is removed from a home, a judge will quickly review the decision—usually within two or three days. You will be told the day and time of the court hearing.

At the first hearing, the judge will decide what to do with your child. Some states call this a *custody* or *detention* hearing. Others call it an *emergency* hearing.

The police officer or social worker who removed your child will explain why your child was removed. She will also tell the judge what the alternatives are for caring for your child. Perhaps a relative can watch your child, or there is room in an emergency shelter.

After the others talk, the judge will give you a chance to explain what happened. You can also suggest how the problem with your child can be solved.

Once the judge has heard from everyone, he will decide where your child will live temporarily. The judge can return your child to you, or decide that your child will remain with someone else.

This decision is not permanent. It only decides where your child will stay until you have an *adjudicatory hearing.*

37

Adjudicatory hearing

An adjudicatory hearing is a trial.

If you've seen trials on TV or in the movies, it may seem different. For one thing, you may not have a jury. In many states, you don't have the automatic right to a jury trial in juvenile matters. It may also be more informal. Often, rules in juvenile court are relaxed.

But make no mistake, at this hearing the judge will decide whether you harmed your child or not.

A lawyer or guardian will often be assigned to represent your child. In some states, you may have a lawyer assigned to represent you. If you are not entitled to a lawyer, you must hire one.

The lawyer working for the state will tell the judge how your child was hurt. She may call witnesses or show the judge pictures or other documents.

The social worker will also speak—describing what is best for your child and how it can be achieved. If she wants you to be reunited with your child, she may suggest that you go to counseling or attend classes.

Your lawyer will also speak, challenging what the others have said, and showing the judge positive aspects of your parenting.

Witnesses

In cases of child abuse, children—even very young children— may be called to testify. This is difficult on everyone, and because children are often frightened in court, they may be videotaped ahead of time, and the videotape shown in court.

In addition to the children, other parents, teachers, doctors, nurses, and daycare workers may testify. It's also common for "expert witnesses"—such as psychologists—to testify.

After the hearing is over, the judge will decide what happened to your child. This is called a *finding of fact.*

The judge may decide right away what to do with your child, or he may wait and decide at a *dispositional hearing.*

Dispositional hearing

The last hearing you have will be a dispositional hearing. This is where the judge makes the permanent decision about what to do with your child.

The judge will either return your child to you, place your child in long-term care in a foster or group home, or terminate your parental rights so your child can be adopted.

As with all other court hearings, you have the right to appeal the decision by the judge if you do not agree with it.

66 You never know how a child will react to a situation where there are many strange people listening to him or her tell an embarrassing story. And you don't know how the child will react to having to tell it in front of the abuser.
Judge Carol Orbison, Juvenile Court 99

You've been falsely accused

During divorce, accusations of child abuse are very common. Every day, judges hear one parent accusing the other of abuse. If you've been falsely accused, you must aggressively defend yourself, or you will lose your children.

Defend yourself

When accused of abuse, many people will assume you did it. To prove otherwise, here are some things you can do:

Get a grip on your emotions. You will feel everything from anger to frustration to desperation. You need to stay calm enough to orchestrate your defense. This is very hard to do, but you must do it.

Attack false statements. If your child made false statements about you, you will be fighting a commonly held belief that "children never lie about abuse." Try to find out if your child was coached or has been alienated from you.

Hire the right lawyer. Don't stick to hiring a lawyer in your area. You'll need a lawyer experienced in fighting abuse accusations—even if he is from outside your court.

Help your lawyer. Help your lawyer do his job by gathering evidence, assembling affidavits attesting to your character, looking up other cases, and checking your court file.

Demand testing. You can demand both independent psychological testing—such as an MMPI-2—and a polygraph test. The polygraph test cannot be used in court, but you can tell everyone you passed.

Don't allow the police or a social worker into your home. As much as you want to cooperate, if you allow law enforcement into your home without a warrant, you waive crucial rights.

Document everything. Follow-up every conversation with a letter stating that 'Failure to confirm or deny within 10 days will constitute an agreement that the information is accurate.'

Should you admit it?

You may be encouraged to admit that you abused your child—even by your own lawyer. It happens all the time. If your lawyer does not believe in you, immediately fire him and hire another lawyer.

66 In recent years, mothers have come into court alleging that their mates have sexually abused their children. It makes the system cower in fear, and the first reaction is usually to cut off a father's visitation rights, 'just to be on the safe side.' Needless to say, this can make ugly domestic disputes even more explosive. I have given custody of children to fathers in most of the cases where mothers persist in making unfounded allegations of sexual abuse. If these women are prepared to torment their children and lie to the court simply to get control in a long-running family dispute, I consider them unfit to parent. *Judge Judy Sheindlin, Don't Pee on My Leg and Tell Me It's Raining: America's Toughest Family Court Judge Speaks Out* 99

A guardian was appointed for your children

When the Judge wants somebody to help him figure out what to do with a child, he may appoint a *guardian ad litem* (GAL) or a *court appointed special advocate* (CASA).

A guardian is a person who represents children in family court and juvenile court. The guardian can be a lawyer, or she may be a specially trained volunteer.

What a guardian does

If a guardian is appointed, she will interview everyone and make her own recommendation about what is best for your children.

The guardian is supposed to:
* Investigate what happened to your child.
* Represent what is best for your child to the Judge.
* Monitor your child after the court hearing.

Some guardians are given complete authority to decide what to do with your children. In those cases, the Judge accepts without question whatever the guardian says.

Other times guardians are asked their opinion, but the Judge balances her advice along with the advice from other professionals—such as a court-appointed psychologist or a social worker.

The guardian does not have to recommend to the court what your child wants, but she is supposed to include your child's wishes when she tells the court what is best for your child.

If the Judge orders you or your spouse to attend classes or follow some kind of a program, the guardian may be the one who monitors to make sure that the orders are followed.

The guardian remains on the case until the Judge releases her or your child becomes an adult.

66 Only the court can appoint CASA volunteers, and only the court can dismiss them if they fail to meet their responsibilities. Ideally, a volunteer is appointed when a child's interests are first threatened and a petition is presented to the court. Typically, the appointment is made during or immediately after the first hearing, which may be a shelter care or custody hearing. *Court Appointed Special Advocates: A Voice for Abused and Neglected Children in Court, Department of Justice* 99

Where to get help

ChildHelp National Child Abuse Hotline
800-422-4453
This number is staffed 24 hours-a-day. Call to speak to a
counselor for a referral to your area.

National Clearinghouse on Child Abuse and Neglect
Information
800-394-3366
www.calib.com/nccanch
Call for information 8:30 am to 5:30 pm (EST). They can
refer you to other organizations that can assist you.

American Humane Society
303-792-9900
www.amerhumane.org
This nonprofit agency works primarily with caseworkers.
They can refer you to a local agency or send you brochures
about child abuse.

National Child Abuse Defense and Resource Center
419-865-0513
If you have been falsely accused, call 9 am to 9 pm (EST) for
referral to an experienced attorney, psychologist, or doctor.

Victims of Child Abuse Laws
303-233-5321
If you have been falsely accused, call 24 hours-a-day to get a
referral for someone in your area.

More reading

Here's a small sample of books on child abuse. Be sure to go online or check your bookstore for more titles.

A Child Called 'It', David J. Pelzer, Health Communications. This heart-wrenching book was written by the survivor of what has been described as "The most severe child abuse case in California."

A Rock and a Hard Place: One Boy's Triumphant Story, Anthony Godby Johnson, Signet, 1994. Compelling story of a boy who was horribly abused, then when he finally escaped, found out he had AIDS.

Ashes to Ashes, Families to Dust, Dean Tong. Compelling book by a man who fought accusations of child abuse. A must-read for anyone falsely accused.

The Courage to Heal, Ellen Bass, Laura Davis (Contributor), Harperperennial, 1994. A comprehensive, supportive, passionate book for survivors, and for those who are the partners, friends, or family members of survivors.

Guilty Until Proven Innocent, Kimberly A. Hart, National Child Abuse Defense and Resource Center. This excellent book has very detailed information for those accused of child abuse. A must-read if you are falsely accused.

The Healing Power of Play: Working With Abused Children, Eliana Gil, Guilford Press, 1999. A professional guide for therapists working with abused children.

The Hostage Child: Sex Abuse Allegations in Custody Disputes, Leora N. Rosen, Michelle Etlin (Contributor), Indiana University Press, 1996. Two child protection activists describe a conspiracy against mothers who make abuse accusations in a divorce.

The Myth of Repressed Memory: False Memories and Allegations of Sexual Abuse, Elizabeth Loftus, Katherine Ketcham, St. Martin's Press, 1996. The bible for combating false accusation based on repressed memory. Loftus is a psychologist who specializes in memory.

Raising Safe Kids in an Unsafe World, Jan Wagner. The author boils down child safety into 30 simple lessons in a bright and easily readable book.

Your children
are missing

You're afraid your children will be kidnapped

During divorce, parents sometimes threaten to "take the kids." This bluff is rarely carried out, but if you're afraid your spouse will do it, you must be prepared.

What is a parental kidnapping?

If your spouse keeps your children from you—that is a *kidnapping.* Depending on where you live and the circumstances, it may also be called an *abduction, child-snatching, custodial interference,* or *child concealment.*

The most common example is when your spouse refuses to give you the children for your visitation, or your spouse refuses to return the children at the end of his visitation.

But it may also be when your spouse moves away with the children without your permission or a court order. Your spouse could stay within the same state, or she might move to another state. Or she might move to another country.

And if your spouse is hiding with the children and you don't know where he is, then you have the additional problem of finding him.

Recognize the warning signs

Parental kidnappings occur when one parent doesn't agree with the arrangements for the children. Your spouse may take the children when:
- She is convinced you are abusing the children and the police will do nothing to stop it.
- He has been frustrated in court and believes he will never get a fair hearing.
- She believes you are "poisoning" the children against her.

Mothers and fathers kidnap almost equally, with most of the "kidnappings" being solved within a few days. But if you think your spouse might take the children, look for the following warning signs:
- Your spouse is angry with the court orders.
- Your spouse believes you are hurting the children.
- Your spouse has threatened to kidnap the children.
- Your spouse just lost custody.
- Your spouse feels you are "turning the children" against her.
- Your children are between three and nine years-old.

If some—or all—of these warning signs are present, take steps now to prevent a kidnapping.

66 Child-snatching is any and all conduct engaged in by either parent in contravention of a valid, proper, existing, and enforceable court order concerning the physical custody of the children of those parents. *Melvin Belli, Divorcing* 99

You need to prevent a kidnapping

If you think your spouse may take the children, do something now. If you act ahead of time, you can prevent a problem. And if your children are kidnapped, you can recover them faster.

Get a custody order

If you do not have a custody order, both parents have equal rights to the children. There is nothing stopping your spouse from moving away with the children.

If you haven't already done so, go to court and ask for a custody order. For around $100, you can hire a paralegal to help you with the paperwork.

By filing papers with the court, you establish *jurisdiction*—the right of the court to decide custody of your children. You can also ask for very specific clauses that describe exactly when your children will be with the other parent.

A custody order can:
- Prevent your spouse from moving away with the children without your permission or the court's approval.
- Require your spouse to pay for an insurance bond guaranteeing that he will return the children.
- Force your spouse to surrender his passport.
- Order the police to assist you in recovering your children.

While a piece of paper will not stop your spouse if he is determined to take the children, a court order can prevent many problems.

Talk to your children

You can also talk to your children about the custody arrangements. You can explain that the schedule cannot be changed without first going to court.

Tell them to call you if there is a problem. Have them memorize your phone number and area code, and work out a "secret code" to use if something has happened.

Tell other people

Once you have a valid custody order, make copies and give it to your children's school, daycare, and the babysitter. If the order includes a restriction on who picks up the children, tell everyone.

Also, talk to the police and tell them your concerns. While the police cannot step in unless there is a problem, ask them for ideas and suggestions. If you think your spouse may leave the country, write to the Passport Office and request that your children not be issued passports without your permission.

And make every effort to talk to your spouse. You may be able to resolve misunderstandings before they escalate into a kidnapping. Parental kidnappings often occur when one parent feels there is no other option. You can provide that other option.

Assemble information

Finally, if you are convinced your spouse will kidnap the children, start collecting information.

In order to recover your children if they are kidnapped, it is crucial that you photograph them, write down their current height and weight, and know their social security numbers.

You can also collect information on your spouse, including his social security number, driver's license number, credit card numbers, and bank account numbers.

And if your spouse has family or friends out-of-state, write down their names, addresses, and phone numbers.

66 You may entertain the fantasy of running away with your children if divorce and custody battles become really bad. Just be sober about this and remember that it's a terrible idea. In the vast majority of parental kidnapping cases, the parent is located and many are convicted of the crime and jailed. Apart from the criminal implications and ramifications, if you take your children and you are found, you will probably never be able to spend unsupervised time with them again. To compound matters, the very person you are trying to keep your children from will probably be awarded placement while you are in jail and, most likely, permanently. *Marc J. Ackerman, "Does Wednesday Mean Mom's House or Dad's?"* 99

Your children have just been kidnapped

If your spouse has taken your child, you must act fast. Every second counts.

Call the police

Call your local police, or call:

911

When you call the police, tell them you need to report a missing child. Give them:
- Your child's name.
- His age.
- A physical description.
- The clothes he was wearing.
- Where you last saw him.
- A recent photograph.

Ask the police to enter your child into the *National Crime Information Center* (NCIC) Missing Person File. This database is maintained by the FBI, and can be accessed by police all over the country.

If the police tell you they must wait 24 hours before they can act–do not accept that. Tell them *The National Child Search Assistance Act of 1990* requires them to act immediately.

If the police still do not cooperate, contact your local FBI office and insist they enter the information into the database. The FBI must take the missing person report from you.

Call a hotline

After calling the police, then call:

800-843-5678

This is the *National Center for Missing and Exploited Children.* It is staffed 24 hours-a-day. The people who answer can help you report your missing child.

Ask the staff to check if your child is entered into the NCIC missing person database. If your child is not listed, ask for instructions on how to get your child into the database.

Contact your state clearinghouse

Look in the appendix of this book to find the phone number for your state missing person clearinghouse. Call that number and tell them what happened.

The staff at the clearinghouse can usually work with police to search for your child within your state. They may also be able to enter your child into the NCIC database.

Call your lawyer

Finally, call your lawyer and tell him your child was taken. If you don't have a lawyer, call the District Attorney. The phone number is in the front of the phone book.

Depending on how your child was taken and what the laws in your state are, you will have several legal tools available.

If you did not have custody when your child was taken, ask your lawyer to file a motion with the court granting you sole custody.

Then, ask the District Attorney to file felony kidnapping charges against your spouse and to issue a felony arrest warrant. However, your spouse can only be charged with a felony if you had a previous custody order and he intentionally violated it.

If you can prove your child was taken out-of-state, you can also ask the D.A. to issue an *Unlawful Flight to Avoid Prosecution* (UFAP) warrant.

Once you've gotten an arrest warrant on your spouse, make sure it's entered into the NCIC missing person database. If your spouse has taken your child out-of-state, the FBI can also help you search for your missing child.

66 Often the act of parental kidnapping is provoked by the breakup of the child's father and mother. Other events that may lead to a parental kidnapping include the actual court filing of divorce papers; the remarriage or serious emotional involvement of one parent with another partner; and conflict over child support, child custody, or visitation. *Just in case... Parental guidelines in case you are considering family separation, National Center for Missing and Exploited Children* **99**

You need to search for your children

To find your child, you have to know where to look. To decide that, you'll gather information and then use it to search for your child.

Interview family and friends

In kidnapping your child, your spouse may have had help from a family member or friend.

Interview everyone you know. Ask if they have seen or know where your child is. If you are not on good terms, give the police a complete list with names, addresses, and telephone numbers. And if someone is uncooperative and you believe he knows something, you maybe able to subpoena him to testify in court.

Gather other information

Your spouse will leave a paper trail, and you can follow that trail to find your child. Here are some things to check:

Airlines, buses, trains, and rental cars. Contact every company to find out if your spouse recently bought tickets or rented a car. Show a photograph of your child to the employees.

Banks, credit cards, and credit bureaus. Check your spouse's bank to see if his money was recently moved. Ask credit card companies for copies of all transactions on your spouse's credit cards. Contact the national credit bureaus to see if your spouse's address has changed. To look at these records, however, you may need to get a court order.

School and birth records. Ask your child's school if his records have been transferred to another school. By law, they must tell you. Also, ask a missing children's organization how to "flag" your child's birth certificate. When your spouse produces your child's birth certificate, you may find him.

Medical records and insurance claims. Ask your child's doctor, dentist, and pharmacy if anyone has requested copies of your child's records. Contact your spouse's insurance carriers to see if his address was changed or coverage was transferred.

Employment records. Contact your spouse's former employer to find out where his pay and benefits are being sent. Ask if any requests for employment references have been made.

Post office. Ask the post office if there is a hold or an address change on your spouse's mail.

Clubs, magazines, and hobbies. Check with organizations your spouse joined in case he changed his address. Contact any magazines and newspapers to see if they are being forwarded.

Telephone records. Check your local phone company and the long-distance companies to see what calls your spouse made before he left. With a proper subpoena, you may also be able to get the records of calls made by his friends and relatives.

Use the parent locator service

You may be able to use the *Federal Parent Locator Service* or your state locator service to find your spouse. These

57

government services access Social Security, IRS, Veterans Administration, and other government files to find someone.

To use the service, an *authorized person* submits a request on your behalf. You have to ask a judge, police officer, district attorney, or FBI agent to help you use the service.

Send out flyers

When you contact the *National Center for Missing and Exploited Children,* ask to have a photograph of your child widely distributed. NCMEC can distribute a poster in your town, your state, around the country, and even internationally.

Tell the media

Call your local newspapers, television stations, and radio stations and tell them what happened. A local reporter may write a story about you. They will need a current photograph of your child and a description of your spouse.

Hire a private investigator

If you want to hire a private investigator, check his references before you sign a contract. Some investigators are honest, but some are not. Almost all of the information an investigator can access is also available to you.

Is your child in another country?

If your spouse has fled the United States, you'll have to search in other countries. An international search is more difficult because a United States custody order has no legal importance in another country.

International kidnappings often involve a foreign citizen who has returned to her country. She may have family and friends in her homeland that make it easier to raise children. And some international kidnappings are by American citizens trying to hide abroad.

Contact the state department

If you believe your spouse has fled the country, contact the U.S. Department of State. This government agency has a division called the *Office of Children's Issues* that handles international kidnappings of American children. The staff works with U.S. embassies world-wide to help you find your child.

At your request, the office can do a "welfare and whereabouts" check on your child in a specific country. After you provide your child's name, date of birth, passport number, and copies of your court orders, a counselor will ask a foreign official to verify your child's residence.

The State Department can also revoke your spouse's passport, making it difficult for him to remain in a foreign country if he is not already a citizen.

The Hague Convention

In 1988, the United States signed the *Hague Convention on the Civil Aspects of International Child Abduction*. This international treaty—approved by more than 40 countries—requires signatory countries to return kidnapped children.

If you believe that your spouse is in a country that has signed the Hague treaty, contact the Office of Children's Issues for help.

Working with bureaucrats

You cannot force a government agency to help you. If you make unreasonable demands, you will alienate people. A better approach is to request that an official listen to your problem and give you assistance. And if the official does not understand his obligations, help him understand so he can help you.

Take care of yourself

When your child was kidnapped, you were hurt. Your feelings of guilt and loss may lead to an inability to sleep, loss of appetite, and severe depression. Some left-behind parents lose their jobs. Others lose their homes.

While searching for your child, make an extra effort to take care of yourself. Sleep and eat properly. Do not let the hurt overwhelm you.

66 Once the child is gone, pain sets in. It is an emptiness that leaves parents wandering around the house and believing they see images of their children. It is hearing the name Daddy or Mommy in a store and thinking it is the missing child calling. It is sitting alone in the child's room, which one keeps just the way it was before the abduction. It is staying in touch with the child's friends so that they will be interested in seeing the child when he or she returns. And, finally, the pain is the thousand little things that remind a parent of a child—a favorite TV show, a song, a book, a favorite color. *Geoffrey Greif and Rebecca Hegar, When Parents Kidnap: The Families Behind the Headlines* 99

You need to recover your children

If you have found your child, you still must get him back. Some parents feel that a kidnapping—a second abduction—is best. However, there are other ways to get your child returned.

Enforce the custody order

If your child is in the United States, you can recover him by asking the police and the local court to enforce your custody order. Here's what to do:

1. If you do not already have one, go to court and get an order awarding you custody of your child.

2. Then, go to the court where your child is located and file a certified copy of your order with the clerk.

3. Next, contact a local lawyer and ask what you must do to have your orders enforced. If you think your spouse will flee again, you can ask a local judge for a "pick up" order returning your child to you.

4. Finally, ask the local police to enforce the custody order. Depending on local law and if a kidnapping warrant exists, the police may or may not arrest your spouse.

5. Be available to take your child when the police act. If you cannot be there, ask a relative or friend to be available.

Kidnap your child

Kidnapping is illegal, but if you are considering this option, at least be aware of the problems.

If your spouse is violent, someone could get hurt. Or the trauma of the re-abduction may make your child want to return to his abductor even after you have recovered him. Or if you fail at the kidnapping, you may be left with no money and your spouse will flee again.

Voluntary return

Another way to get your child back is by negotiating. *Child Find of America* offers a mediation service to help with voluntary recoveries, and they report some success.

If your child is in another country

If you've found your child in another country, you'll have to work with that government to get your child back.

Use the State Department

If the foreign country has signed the Hague treaty, the staff of the Office of Children's Issues in the State Department can help you fill out the application. They can also give you vital information about the laws and customs of the country, provide you with the names of local lawyers and interpreters, and help you authenticate documents.

Though the State Department cannot "grab" your child for you, they can help you coordinate your legal efforts to get your child back.

File a civil action

Even though a U.S. custody order is not binding on a foreign government, you may be able to recover your child through a foreign court proceeding.

To do that, you'll have to hire a foreign lawyer, have documents translated, authenticated, and filed with the foreign court. Then you'll have to travel to the country to make your case.

File a criminal action or revoke passport

You may also be able to recover your child by getting a kidnapping warrant on your spouse, and then asking the foreign government to extradite him back to the U.S.

Or, you can try to force your spouse back to the United States by asking the U.S. passport office to revoke his passport. If he does not have dual citizenship, this will make him an undocumented alien, and the other country may deport him.

66 Some searching parents are able to turn all their intense emotions into an aggressive energy that they funnel into productive search efforts. Some start out strong, then slowly become exasperated by the system, failures and disappointments. Still others are so distraught that they are unable to hold down jobs, have successful relationships, or even begin to coordinate recovery efforts. *Maureen Dabbagh, The Recovery of Internationally Abducted Children: A Comprehensive Guide* 99

Your spouse is moving away

In a divorce, it's very common for one parent to want to move away. She may wish to be closer to her family, or he may want to start a new job in another state.

If the noncustodial parent wants to move, he may simply see less of his children. But if the custodial parent wants to move, her moving away may dramatically lessen the time the noncustodial parent has with his children.

Get a custody order

If you do not have a custody order, either parent can move. Until a court says differently, you both have equal rights to live where you want with your children.

If you want to stop your spouse from moving, you have to go to court and ask the judge for a *temporary custody order.* This will say where the children will live and who will have primary custody.

Get a restraining order

To stop your spouse from moving, you must also ask for a *restraining order.* This will prevent your spouse from relocating with the children.

The judge may grant this—or he may not. The laws about moving away are constantly changing, and getting a restraining order depends on who your judge is and what has happened with recent cases that have been appealed.

Bargain with your spouse

Sometimes a spouse demanding to move away is really just bargaining in the divorce. If you think your spouse is trying to extract a better divorce settlement, you'll have to weigh your desire to be with your children against whatever it is your spouse wants.

Follow your spouse

Finally, if you cannot keep your spouse from moving away, a last resort may be for you to follow her and live nearby so you can continue to see your children.

This may not be easy, but it may be your only choice if you want to see your children.

66 The judge granted me physical custody of Brian. Mike received liberal visitation rights, yet this still angered him so much that, on several occasions, he threatened to take our son away from me. Concerned, I reported the threats to the judge, but he said that nothing could be done unless Mike actually acted on his threats... A week after the divorce became final, Mike came to pick up Brian for the weekend. He didn't return on Sunday evening, and no one answered the phone at the rooming house where he was staying. *'Welcome Home, Brian,' Ladies' Home Journal* 99

Your spouse won't let you see the children

When you first separate, you may have an informal agreement for sharing the children. This agreement may work fine—or it may not. Without a court order, your spouse can control when and how often you see your children.

If you are having problems, you must go to court and ask the judge to create a *detailed visitation order.* Then you must enforce that order.

Get a detailed custody order

If you don't have a custody order, or if you have one but it only specifies *reasonable* visitation, you must go to court and ask for a detailed custody order.

You can ask the judge to state exactly which days and times you have the children. The order can account for all the different parts of the year—the school year, the summer, and holidays. The order can even include penalties if your spouse doesn't cooperate.

Sample visitation schedule

Here's some sample language for a detailed custody order:

School year. "On alternate weeks Mother shall drop off the minor child with Father at 6 pm on Friday, and Father shall

66

return minor child at 6 pm on Sunday. During any weekends where there is an attached holiday, the party having custody on that weekend shall have the holiday attached."

Holiday. "Mother shall have the minor child during the Christmas vacation from Friday before vacation with return to school on the day school resumes in all odd numbered years. Father shall have the exact same period in all even numbered years."

Enforce the court order

Once you have a detailed order, you must adhere to it, and so must your spouse. If your spouse refuses, you can call the police. Show the police a copy of the order and ask them to enforce the order. They may tell your spouse to turn over the children or she will be arrested.

If the police will not arrest your spouse or make her give you the children, you can still return to court and ask the judge to hold your spouse in *contempt of court.* This is a serious violation, and if your spouse is found guilty, she can be punished in many ways, including losing custody of the children.

66 Often, parents not living with their children question where they should take the children and what they should plan in the way of amusement for them, particularly if the children are young. Activities may add to the pleasure of the time together, but most important is the parent's involvement with the children. A giving of self is more important than whatever material things they may get. *Parents Are Forever, Association of Family and Conciliation Courts* 99

67

Your spouse doesn't visit the children

After divorce, children often live with one parent, and the other parent is granted *visitation.* If your spouse does not visit his children, you must help your children cope with the disappointment they feel.

Why parents stop visiting

When you were living together, your spouse saw his children as often as he wanted. But after you broke up, he was restricted in seeing his children. Indeed, in many custody orders, he can only see his children four days a month.

This minimal amount of time makes it impossible to be a meaningful parent. For many noncustodial parents—both men and woman—it becomes easier to simply give up and walk away, rather than try to be a parent in a schedule that makes it impossible.

How your children feel

When your spouse doesn't show up for his visitation, your children will know. They may show their hurt and disappointment, or they may not. Perhaps they simply shrug and say "It doesn't matter." It does.

Children of divorce will often talk about a parent not coming to see them for the rest of their lives. The hurt runs that deep.

Talk to your children

If your spouse does not visit, you must talk to your children. They may think they were bad or they're somehow to blame. You will have to work very hard to persuade them they didn't do anything wrong.

If you can afford it, bring your children to a divorce support group or private counseling. Even young children can benefit from play therapy with a child psychologist.

Talk to your spouse

You must also talk to your spouse. You may not feel like it, or you may feel that your communication with him is poor, but only by talking to your spouse will you discover what the problem is.

Perhaps the custody order can be changed to solve the problem. Or perhaps you are subtly discouraging him from visiting and you're not aware of it.

As difficult as it may be to talk to your spouse, the hurt your children are feeling will last the rest of their lives. You must do something about it.

66 A great many visiting fathers, angered and ultimately defeated by the realization that they are reduced to becoming visitors in their children's lives, simply give up the effort and withdraw completely from their children's lives. *David Blankenhorn, Fatherless America* 99

You're afraid your children will run away

Children leave home for many reasons. While most children runaway because of family problems, some leave because of peer pressure. If you think your child might runaway, watch for the warning signs, then do something about it.

Recognize the warning signs

You should be concerned if your child:
- Talks about running away.
- Withdraws from family and friends.
- Is having problems in school.
- Is being abused in the family.

While there are many reasons a child will leave, look for changes that something is wrong with your child. If you think something is wrong, then something *is* wrong. Trust your judgment.

What to do if your child has run away

If you cannot stop your child from running away, act quickly to recover your child. First, call the police:

911

When you talk to the police, give them the same information as if your child was kidnapped. Tell the police your child's age, a physical description, his clothes, and so on. When you call the police, be prepared to give them a recent photograph of your child.

Then, call your child's friends, relatives, and neighbors. Children usually go to someone they know, and you may be able to find your child that way.

If that doesn't work, call a hotline:

800-843-5678

The *National Center for Missing and Exploited Children* is staffed 24 hours-a-day and can take a report on your child. Also, look in the *Where to get help* section for other numbers to call.

Act quickly

The first 48 hours are crucial. Your child faces many dangers when he runs away, and you must act quickly to prevent her from being hurt.

❝ Running away can be a frightening experience—for both the child and the parents. Your child becomes vulnerable as soon as he or she leaves home—potentially falling victim to drugs, drinking, crime, sexual exploitation, child pornography, or child prostitution. In the face of this, many parents may feel guilty or depressed... or even paralyzed by fear. *Just in case... Parental guidelines in case your child might someday be a runaway, National Center for Missing and Exploited Children* ❞

Where to get help

Abductions within the United States

National Center for Missing and Exploited Children
800-843-5678
www.missingkids.org
This number is staffed 24 hours-a-day. Call to report a
missing child. NCMEC is the main organization for tracking
and recovering missing children.

Federal Bureau of Investigation
(202) 324-2000
Call this Washington, D.C., number for general information
and the number of your local office. You can also find out
how to get an *Unlawful Flight to Avoid Prosecution* warrant on
your spouse.

U.S. Department of Health and Human Services
Office of Child Support Enforcement
Federal Parent Locator Service
202-401-9267
The FPLS can help you locate a parent who has kidnapped
your children. Call to find out how you can access the state
and federal locators.

Child Find of America
800-426-5678
These counselors help parents who are thinking about
abducting their children. They also refer callers to crisis lines
and legal experts.

Missing Children HELP Center
800-872-5437
Call to report a missing child. This organization maintains a database of the procedures in each state for locating missing children.

Child Search
800-832-3773
www.childsearch.org

Abductions outside the United States

National Center for Missing and Exploited Children
800-843-5678 (in the U.S.)
001-703-522-9320 (outside the U.S.)
www.missingkids.org
The hotline is staffed with bilingual operators who can handle more than 140 languages. Call 8 am to 8 pm Monday–Friday, and 12 pm to 8 pm, Saturday, Sunday, and holidays (EST).

U.S. Department of State
Office of Children's Issues
202-736-7000
travel.state.gov
If your child is in a country that has signed the Hague Treaty, this office can initiate hearings that will require the other country to honor the treaty. They can also check to make sure your child is safe.

U.S. Department of State
Office of Passport Services
202-326-6168
If you have an arrest warrant for your spouse, this office can revoke his passport.

Vanished Children's Alliance National Headquarters
800-826-4743
Call this non-profit organization to register missing children,
to receive help with law enforcement agencies, to distribute
missing children flyers, and for counseling and emotional
support.

ICANN: International Child Abduction Attorney Network
202-662-1740
This network is being managed by the American Bar
Association Center on Children and the Law.

Child Quest International
408-287-4673
www.childquest.org

Runaways

National Runaway Switchboard
800-621-4000
www.nrscrisisline.org
Call for information and crisis counseling. Runaways can
find out about shelter, counseling, and transportation.

National Youth Crisis Hotline
800-448-4663
www.ydi.org
Call this crisis hotline for information and referrals.

More reading

Here are some titles for books and brochures on parental kidnappings. For some excellent free information, contact the *National Center for Missing and Exploited Children.*

Family Abduction: How to Prevent an Abduction and What to Do If Your Child Is Abducted, Hoff, P., National Center for Missing and Exploited Children. Contains information on the UCCJA, PKPA, Hague Convention, and the International Child Abduction Remedies Act of 1988.

International Child Abductions: A Guide to Applying the 1988 Hague Convention, with forms, De Hart, Section of Family Law, American Bar Association, 1993. Explains the convention.

Just in case... Guidelines for military families in case your child is the victim of parental kidnapping. The National Center for Missing and Exploited Children. A brochure.

Just in case... Guidelines on using the Federal Parent Locator Service in cases of parental kidnapping and child custody. The National Center for Missing and Exploited Children. A brochure. Detailed information about the use of the Federal Parent Locator Service.

Just in case... Parental guidelines in case your child is testifying in court. The National Center for Missing and Exploited Children. A brochure. Helpful information if your child is called to testify as a witness.

Just in case... Parental guidelines in finding professional help in case your child is missing or the victim of sexual abuse or exploitation. The

National Center for Missing and Exploited Children. Another helpful brochure.

Missing and Abducted Children: A Law Enforcement Guide to Case Investigation and Program Management. The National Center for Missing and Exploited Children. A brochure. For law enforcement officers, explains the difference between enforcing child custody orders and enforcing arrest warrants for parental kidnappers.

Obstacles to the Recovery and Return of Parentally Abducted Children, L.K. Girdner and P.M. Hoff, United States Department of Justice, 1994. Prepared for the DOJ's Office of Juvenile Justice.

Selected State Legislation: A Guide for Effective State Laws to Protect Children. The National Center for Missing and Exploited Children. A brochure. A list of states with laws protecting a noncustodial parent's access to their children. Contains recently enacted law reforms affecting missing children.

The Recovery of Internationally Abducted Children: A Comprehensive Guide, Maureen Dabbagh, McFarland & Company, 1997. A terrific manual about the recovery of children kidnapped to destinations outside the U.S., written by an experienced expert witness and lecturer on the topic. Dabbagh's own two-year-old daughter was kidnapped to Syria in 1992 and abandoned there by her father.

When Parents Kidnap: The Families Behind the Headlines, G. Grief and R. Hegar, Free Press, 1993. Studies of parental kidnappings and the effect on everyone involved.

You're angry or depressed

You can't control your anger

You will feel angry during your divorce. And you will feel angry after your divorce. *Everyone* feels that way.

But what you do with your anger is up to you. You can either let it take over your life, or you can use it in ways that help you. It's up to you.

Are you angry?

The most common forms of anger are easy to spot. You know you're angry if you've physically hit your spouse. During an argument, you may have kicked her, or slapped her, or shoved her. You also know you're angry if you criticize your spouse with name-calling or accusations.

But you may also show your anger in more subtle ways. Maybe you feel irritable all the time and you can't quite figure out why. Or you're jealous of your spouse, or you're rigid and unforgiving, or you're become sullen and uncommunicative.

In short, you may be angry, but express it in other ways. Anger prevents you from feeling good about yourself and others—even if you don't recognize it as anger.

And if you've been angry for a long time, you may have created some very sophisticated ways to hide or "cover up" your anger.

Manage your anger

Here are some simple techniques you can use to manage your anger. Some are things you should *avoid* doing, while others are things you should *start* doing. Use the techniques that work best for you.

Avoid things that make you angry. You know what makes you mad, so stay away. This works best if you can avoid a particular person or situation. Of course, that's not always possible.

Reduce things that make you angry. If you see something coming that will make you angry, step in and "cut it off." Be assertive and control what makes you angry.

Reduce support for your anger. If you've got a friend or family member who encourages you to be angry—don't talk to them. Your "friend" is not helping you.

Eliminate angry fantasies. You may replay something that gets you angry, or you may fantasize about revenge. When you find yourself doing that, consciously think about something else instead.

Vent your anger in a safe way. Punch a pillow, cry, scream— whatever exhausts your anger can help. Abraham Lincoln used to write down what made him angry and then tear up the paper.

Change how you show your anger. You can change what you do when you get angry. The next time something makes you mad, respond calmly, or do nothing at all. Or even better, use the energy to do something good for you. Then, every time you get angry, you'll be improving your life.

Empathize with the other person. Put yourself in the other person's shoes. Maybe he's scared, or sick, or he doesn't know he's making you angry. You'll reduce your own anger if you see the world as he sees it.

Help yourself. If you feel better, you'll be less angry by what others do. Go on a diet, return to school—anything that makes you feel good about yourself. Meditation and yoga have been used for centuries to reduce anger.

Forgive. Choosing to forgive allows you to open your heart and love again. This sounds so simple—and it is. Forgiveness is always within you.

❝ Every little thing blows up in your face. You can't escape the rage, the urge to kill. Separation and divorce release a stockpile of anger between the spouses that has been repressed over the years during the marriage. Your fury erupts suddenly, like a geyser of oil. You scream at each other now, you scream and kick, you smash glasses on the floor. Your arguments are venomous... *Abigail Trafford, Crazy Time: Surviving Divorce and Building a New Life* ❞

You're tired or run down

It's easy to let yourself go during divorce. Dealing with the stresses of divorce makes it difficult to eat right and sleep right.

If you're tired or run down, now is the time to take care of yourself. And when you do, you'll find that managing your divorce is easier.

Are you tired or run down?

You know you're having problems if you:
- Have trouble getting to sleep.
- Don't sleep well or you have nightmares.
- Wake up tired in the morning.
- Feel exhausted all day.
- Get a lot of colds.
- Get a lot of headaches or backaches.
- Have indigestion, constipation, diarrhea, or heartburn.
- Have muscle tension, swelling, or inflammation in your joints.
- Have aches and pains that don't go away.
- Have a menstrual period that lasts too long.

Of course, there are many signs of stress, and many things can make you feel "out of it." The important thing is to trust your feelings. If you think something is wrong, make an extra effort to take better care of yourself.

Eat right

You start taking care of yourself by eating a well-balanced diet. That means eating the right types of foods and in the right amounts. A balanced diet provides protein and complex carbohydrates while containing only moderate amounts of sodium, fats, and simple sugars.

How do you eat a balanced diet? It's simple. When you go shopping, *buy healthy foods.* Then, when it's time to cook dinner or pack a lunch, you'll find something healthy in your refrigerator. That means loading up the shopping cart with fruits, vegetables, and gains, and leaving off the sugars and fats.

This isn't a foolproof system—you can still pick up junk food everywhere—but it's a start. And it doesn't take a lot of effort.

Sleep right

Sleep problems are so common, it's easy to ignore this essential part of your health. But the fatigue or drowsiness or apathy you feel because you didn't get enough sleep affects everything you do. Here are some strategies to overcoming sleep problems.

Make a schedule. You can actually train yourself to get to sleep if you go to bed at the same time every night, and wake up at the same time every morning. No exceptions. It's hard to do at first, but it really works!

Make a place. Chance are, you have a TV in your bedroom, a telephone, book, magazines, and you bring things to eat into bed. Whoa! Get rid of the stuff around your bed. Make your bedroom just that—a room with a bed.

Eat right. Food changes how you feel, and if you want to use it to help you, avoid caffeine and alcohol and try a light carbohydrate snack just before bedtime.

Relax. Just before bedtime, take a bath, do yoga, meditate—use any relaxation technique you like. They can all work.

Exercise

No matter how well you eat and sleep, you still need to exercise. The American College of Sports Medicine recommends exercising at least three times a week.

When you exercise, you should work hard enough to get your heart beating at 60% to 90% of your maximum rate. To calculate your maximum heart rate, subtract your age from 220. For example, a 35 year-old would have a maximum heart rate of 185, and an exercise range of 111 to 166.

It doesn't matter what you do—walking, swimming, free weights, tennis, and so on—as long as you get your heart going.

66 A good place to start an effective stress-reduction program is to find out where you hold stress in your body. Lie down with your eyes closed. Take the phone off the hook and tell everyone you don't want to be disturbed for an hour. Then scan your body from the tips of your toes to the top of your head, looking for places where you hold tension, then consciously letting that tension go. *Diana Shepherd* 99

You're depressed

Divorce brings out many feelings—anger, frustration, fear, and sometimes—depression. While it's common to feel depressed during your divorce, you don't have to let it take over your life. You can control it.

Are you depressed?

You know you're depressed if you:
- Feel worthless or empty.
- Feel everything is hopeless and you can't change things.
- Take drugs or drink too much.
- Have considered suicide.
- Are always tired. You don't sleep well, and you don't wake up refreshed.
- Feel irritable or sad for no reason. Little things upset you. You cry without knowing why.
- Have persistent aches. You may have a headache, stomachache, backache, or abdominal pains.
- Can't concentrate or remember things. You don't "get things done."
- Don't enjoy food, or you take comfort in food. You may gain or lose a lot of weight.

As you look over the list, realize that everyone has experienced some of these symptoms. That doesn't mean everyone is depressed. It simply means feeling "down" at times is normal.

But if you feel depressed more than a few weeks, then your depression may be deepening into an illness. A very serious illness. And you need help

Get help

You can't fight depression by yourself. You must get help.

The most effective treatment is a combination of medicine and therapy. The medicine corrects the chemical imbalance in your brain that is causing the depression, and the therapy helps you cope with the problems in your life.

Take medication

If you're depressed, talk to a doctor. Ask him to prescribe something to treat the depression. The doctor will prescribe an *antidepressant.*

Antidepressants work by changing the chemistry in your brain that creates depression. They are not addictive, but they do have side effects, like dry mouth or drowsiness.

If you are given medicine, such as Zoloft or Prozac, you may have to take it for as little as a few months, or for many years. You will have to take your "meds" on a regular schedule—not just when you feel like it.

The medication will have no effect if you are not truly depressed. But if you are, the medicine can help you get your life "back to normal."

Start therapy

Along with medication, you will need therapy. Find a psychologist who can treat you. The psychologist can use several different therapies to help you fight the depression. You can find a psychologist in *Where to get help.*

The psychologist may use *cognitive therapy* to help you change your thinking and your perception of your environment. Or he may use *interpersonal therapy* to help you interact successfully with your family, friends, and coworkers.

Therapy is designed to improve your "social skills" so you can cope more effectively with the stresses in your life.

Find support

In addition to medication and therapy, you can also talk to other people who are depressed. It's very helpful to know you "are not alone." Depression is common, and others have successfully fought it.

To find a support group, ask your doctor or therapist, and read *You're looking for a support group.*

   Depressive illnesses are not due to personal weakness or a character flaw, but are biological illnesses related to imbalanced or disrupted brain chemistry. The brain is an organ of the body and can get sick just like the heart, liver, or kidneys. A combination of genetic, psychological, and environmental factors all play a role in how and when a depressive illness may manifest itself. Depression can appear out of nowhere, when everything is going fine, at a time when there would be no reason for a person to feel depressed. *SA/VE: Suicide Awareness Voices of Education*

You're thinking about suicide

If your pain is so deep that you can't see a way out, you may be thinking of killing yourself. If you are, realize the crisis will pass. You can be treated. You can get help.

Are you thinking about suicide?

Here are some warning signs you're thinking about suicide:
- You're talking or writing about it. You say things like "Everyone would be better off without me." or "I won't be around much longer." or "I can't see any way out."
- You're visiting or calling people to say goodbye.
- You're giving away your things or making final arrangements. You may have recently made or revised your will.
- You're suddenly happier or calmer—anticipating that your problems will soon be over.
- You're hurting yourself. You may be abusing alcohol or drugs, or you're driving recklessly. You may have had some recent close calls or accidents.
- You've tried it before. You've made some previous attempts. You're working up to it.
- You're creating a plan. You're setting the time and the way that you'll do it.

If something bad has just happened, you may be close to suicide. If you're in a crisis, you're having a problem *now,* and you don't see a reason to keep on living.

What you should know

You can get help. You are not alone. There are people who care about you and will listen to you and help you.

What you are feeling is the result of an illness. This illness can be treated with medication. If you have some medicine, it may not be working. You may need something else.

This is a temporary crisis. No matter how bad it is today, it will get better. Maybe tomorrow, maybe after that. You can't see that right now, but it will.

Call a hotline

If you are thinking about suicide, call a suicide hotline. Look in your phone book, or call:

800-784-2433

This is the *National Suicide Hotline.* It is staffed 24 hours a day. You can talk to a counselor anonymously.

You can also call your doctor or go to a hospital emergency room. The important thing is that you are not alone.

What else you can do

Getting past a crisis is only the beginning. You must get long-term help.

You may need to be admitted to a hospital. You are in pain, and you can get better in a hospital. In a hospital, your medication can monitored to make sure it works.

88

You may also need to talk to a counselor. Talking will not solve your problems, but a counselor can teach you better coping skills.

You must also strengthen your reasons to live. Family, religion, love of nature—focus on things that are important to you and give you a reason to stay alive.

Finally, you must give up drinking or using drugs. You are ill, and abusing substances is making it worse. To get back to normal, you must get healthy.

No one wants so much pain that the only way out is suicide. But you can find a solution. You can feel good again.

" If you are unable to think of solutions other than suicide, it is not that solutions don't exist, only that you are currently unable to see them. Although it might seem as if your unhappiness will never end, it is important to realize that crises are usually time-limited. Solutions are found, feelings change, unexpected positive events occur. Don't let suicide rob you of better times that would have come your way, if only more time had been allowed to pass. *American Association of Suicidology* "

You're drinking or using drugs

If you take drugs or drink too much, you're not alone. Many people do it. But abusing substances hurts you, and if you want to stop, you have to take the first step.

Do you have a substance abuse problem?

Before you can help yourself, you have to understand there is a problem. You have a substance abuse problem if:
- You've already tried to stop, and you can't do it.
- You have legal-related problems, such as a DUI.
- You have health-related problems, such as blackouts or your hands shake.
- The amount you use has been increasing over the years.
- You use multiple drugs to "even out" the effect.
- You only go to parties where you can drink or take drugs.
- You're having trouble at work, or you miss a lot of work.
- All your money goes to buying drugs.
- You need something when you first wake up.

Deep down, you may already know you have a problem. Maybe you don't want to admit it because it will make you look "weak." Or maybe you're too afraid to admit it because you know what it really means.

But if you are abusing substances, you have an illness, and it will only get worse until you do something about it.

Get help

It takes courage to get help. But the sooner you do it, the easier it will be. And when you do ask for help, you'll find there are a lot of people who can help you.

If you belong to a church, a minister or rabbi can help. Or, you may want to talk to counselor or therapist. Or your employer may have an employee assistance program (EAP) available that provides free or low-cost counseling.

Call a hotline

If you're not sure where to start, call this number:

800-729-6686

This is the *National Clearinghouse for Alcohol and Drug Information.* You can get information on different drugs and how they affect you. You can also get information on treatment programs.

Also, look in your phone book under "alcohol" or "drug abuse" for the numbers of community and social service agencies. And finally, call the numbers in the *Where to get help* section.

Check into a hospital

If your chemical dependency is severe, you may need to enroll in an inpatient program such as *Hazelden* or *Betty Ford.* Most programs last for three to five weeks, and are designed to get you past the immediate withdrawal from your addiction.

To find a program, call the hotlines listed in the *Where to get help* section.

Join a self-help group

When it comes to substance abuse, there are many self-help groups available. The best known for alcohol abuse— *Alcoholics Anonymous* and *Al-Anon*—may have a chapter near you. But there are also groups for drug abuse, including *Narcotics Anonymous* and *Cocaine Anonymous.*

When you look around, you'll realize there are treatment centers all over the place. And if you can't find a local chapter, you may be able to start one.

Attend meetings

Once you join a group, you'll attend meetings with other people who have the same problem you do.

By going to these meetings, you first attack your dependence on the drug, and then learn how to avoid returning to the drug. You won't be "cured" by going to a meeting, but you can be taught how to control your addiction.

Self-help groups such as *Alcoholics Anonymous* work because members in recovery teach each other what it takes to recover. They also provide information on the particular problems with the drug.

By the way, if you are ordered by the court to join a group, you can usually get a "proof of attendance" that will satisfy the judge.

Help yourself

You don't want to depend on alcohol or drugs for the rest of your life. You can cut back. Here are some ways how.

Break the habit. Don't take anything when you feel angry or alone. Instead, go to a movie or out to dinner.

Avoid temptations. Don't keep anything at home. And stay away from people or places where you're encouraged to drink or take drugs.

Say no. If you must deal with people who use substances, do not participate. If they give you a hard time—avoid them.

Talk to someone. If you're feeling stressed and you've joined a self-help group, call a friend. Otherwise, call a hotline.

66 If you drink to change the way you feel; to relieve boredom, anxiety, depression, anger, or low self-esteem; to gain acceptance form others; to escape life's problems; or to feel part of the good life you see in alcohol advertising, then you are not alone. These are the reasons many people give for drinking. But figuring out why you began drinking or using other drugs is not important right now. What is important is to recognize that alcohol and/or other drugs are taking you away from the life you want, understanding how serious the problem is, and then getting help. *National Clearinghouse for Alcohol and Drug Information* 99

93

You're looking for a support group

As you go through a divorce, you'll realize divorce is a *process*, not an *event*. That means you need time to adjust to life after divorce. And the longer you were married, the more you have to adjust.

To get some help working through your "emotional divorce," you can join a *support group*.

Decide what you want

Many divorce support groups are run by a professional counselor, but some are led by the members themselves.

Since there are many different kinds of groups, first decide what you want out of a group, then go looking for it. Do you want the group to:
- Provide information?
- Provide emotional support?
- Provide access to services—such as a lawyer or a psychologist?
- Have a prerequisite for joining?
- Have a restriction on who can join—such as only women or only men?
- Meet often—such as weekly or bi-weekly?
- Have meetings that are close to where you live or work?
- Allow members to socialize outside the meetings?
- Require members to commit to a minimum amount of time—such as 10 weeks or six months?

Find the right group

Once you've decided what you want, look around and see what's available. You may not find exactly what you want, but you may find something worthwhile.

Here are some places to look:

Friends. Your friends aren't the most objective people in the world, but you may have a friend who knows about the perfect support group for you.

Church. Virtually every church either has a divorce support group, or knows where one is.

Phone book. The front of your phone book will have local helplines. Call and ask about groups in your area.

Online. No matter what problem you have, you're sure to find a group on the internet. To find a group, go to a major search engine—such as Yahoo!—and look it up. Also, be sure to check out good divorce web sites, including *DivorceNet* and *Divorce Source.* They have links to many other divorce-related web sites.

66 A self-help group can be any number of things. It can be a group of people getting together to share information. It can be a group led by a trained facilitator, or a group managed by members of the group itself. The bottom line is that a self-help group is a forum for people who have "been there" to get together, share experiences, solve problems, and share resources. Participating in a self-help group can help you regain your emotional center. *Divorce Magazine* 99

Where to get help

National Clearinghouse for Alcohol and Drug Information
800-729-6686
www.health.org
This government agency answers questions about alcohol
and substance abuse prevention, intervention, and treatment.
They can handle crisis calls and can refer you to a hotline or
local treatment center.

Substance Abuse & Mental Health Services Administration
(SAMHSA)
800-662-4357
www.samhsa.gov
Use the interactive map on this government web site to find a
substance abuse treatment program anywhere in the country.

National Council on Alcoholism and Drug Dependence
800-622-2255
Call to find a local treatment center, or leave your address to
receive information about alcohol and drug abuse.

American Council on Alcoholism
800-527-5344
Call Monday through Friday for referral to a local treatment
center.

Alcoholics Anonymous
212-647-1680
212-870-3400
www.alcoholics-anonymous.org
This organization will help you recover from alcoholism.
Call to find a local meeting.

Al-anon/Alateen
800-344-2666
800-356-9996
For help with alcoholism for a friend or family member. Call
to find a local meeting.

800-ALCOHOL
800-252-6465
Call for referral to a local treatment program.

800-COCAINE
800-262-2463
Call for referral to a local treatment program.

888-MARIJUANA
888-627-4582
Call for referral to a local treatment program.

800-SUICIDE
800-784-2433
Call this national hotline if you are considering suicide.

American Association of Suicidology
202-237-2280
www.suicidology.org
Check this web site to get helpful information on suicide, and
for the phone number and address of a local crisis center or
support group.

American Foundation for Suicide Prevention
800-573-4433
800-269-1014
www.afsp.org
Call to get a free depression screening and a referral for
further evaluation.

Suicide Awareness Voices of Education (SA/VE)
612-946-7998
www.save.org
Go to this web site for helpful information on depression and suicide.

National Alliance for the Mentally Ill
800-950-6264
www.nami.org
The helpline provides information and referrals to support groups around the country. Call Monday through Friday.

National Mental Health Association
www.nmha.org
800-969-6642
Call on weekdays for information on mental health topics and referrals to doctors.

American Association of Marriage and Family Therapy
www.aamft.org
800-374-2638
Call for referral to a therapist.

Divorce Net
www.divorcenet.com
A well-established site with state-by-state resources, bulletin boards, reading room, and more.

Divorcesource
www.divorcesource.com
A good site with helpful links, a message center, chat rooms, a bookstore, and more.

More reading

There are literally thousands of books on anger, depression, stress, and substance abuse. Here are some good ones.

60 Second Stress Management: The Quickest Way to Relax and Ease Anxiety, Andrew Goliszek, New Horizon Press, 1992. Everything you need to manage stress quickly and effectively.

The Angry Heart: Overcoming Borderline and Addictive Disorders, Joseph Santoro, Ronald Cohen, New Harbinger, 1997. Help for people with addictions and personality disorders.

The Angry Self: A Comprehensive Approach to Anger Management, Miriam Gottlieb, Zeig, Tucker & Theisen, 1999. This clearly written book is filled with tools to manage anger.

Breaking the Patterns of Depression, Michael Yapco, Main Street Books, 1998. A clinical psychologist offers one hundred exercises to control depression.

Choosing to Live: How to Defeat Suicide Through Cognitive Therapy, Thomas Ellis, Cory Newman, New Harbinger, 1996. A book for preventing suicide with proven therapy techniques.

Crazy Time: Surviving Divorce and Building a New Life, Abigail Trafford, HarperPerennial, 1993. Trafford weaves her own experiences with well-written insights about divorce.

The Dance of Anger: A Woman's Guide to Changing the Patterns of Intimate Relationships, Harriet Lerner, HarperCollins, 1997. A bestseller that shows women how to turn anger into a constructive force for reshaping their lives.

The Depression Workbook: A Guide for Living With Depression and Manic Depression, Mary Ellen Copeland, Matthew McKay (Contributor), New Harbinger, 1992. Insights, experiences, and strategies for living with extreme mood swings.

Night Falls Fast: Understanding Suicide, Kay Redfield Jamison, Knopf, 1999. A psychiatry professor discusses suicide and how to prevent it. Very compelling.

Out of the Nightmare: Recovery from Depression and Suicidal Pain, David Conroy, New Liberty, 1991. A book about suicide from the executive director of Suicide Prevention Resources in New York City.

Rational Recovery: The New Cure for Substance Addiction, Jack Trimpey, Pocket Books, 1996. A self-recovery program for alcoholism and drug addiction.

Relaxation & Stress Reduction Workbook, Martha Davis, Elizabeth Robbins Eshelman, Matthew McKay, New Harbinger, 1998. A social worker and a clinical therapist describe stress reduction methods, from hypnosis and meditation to biofeedback and assertiveness training.

Seven Weeks to Sobriety, Joan Larsen, Loan Larson, Fawcett, 1997. A book from the Health Recovery Center in Minnesota challenges the notion that alcoholism recovery programs work.

Undoing Depression: What Therapy Doesn't Teach You and Medication Can't Give You, Richard O'Connor, Berkley, 1999. A psychotherapist describes how to beat depression by adopting an effective set of life skills.

Your money is gone

You need to protect your money

When you were married, you shared your money and combined your assets. But now that you're getting a divorce, you have to separate your money and protect your assets.

Joint credit cards, joint checking accounts, safe deposit boxes, brokerage accounts—these are a few of the many types of assets you have to protect during divorce.

Close joint accounts

Until you get a court order preventing him, there is nothing stopping your spouse from withdrawing everything in your joint accounts and charging the joint credit cards to the limit.

The simplest way to protect your money is to close all the joint accounts. These may include:
- Checking accounts.
- Savings accounts.
- Brokerage accounts.
- Major credit cards.
- Store and gasoline cards.
- Credit lines.

If your financial life is complex, you may have many different assets, even cash in a whole life insurance policy! Now that you're getting a divorce, you must close the joint accounts and secure the shared assets, or you will be responsible for what your spouse does.

Raid safe deposit box

If you have a safe deposit box, it probably has valuable things in it, such as important papers, jewelry, or cash.

To protect your assets, photograph the contents of the box or take an inventory. And make sure a witness signs the inventory. But if you think that won't be enough, then remove the contents for safekeeping. Of course, if you do that, your spouse may accuse you of stealing, so you'll have to be able to prove you did nothing wrong.

Stash cash

Divorce is expensive, and you'll certainly need money. If your accounts will be frozen, plan ahead of time by withdrawing as much cash as possible from your marital accounts and then keeping the money in a secure place. Set aside three to six months of "liquid" funds.

Get an injunction

Another way to protect your assets is to go to court and ask for a *property injunction.*

An injunction is nothing more than a judge ordering somebody not to do something. You can ask a judge to prevent the removal, sale, transfer, or other use of a particular asset during the divorce. You can "freeze" bank accounts, brokerage accounts, the title to real property—just about anything.

Once you've gotten an injunction, send a copy to the bank or brokerage house where the account is located. The injunction will keep the assets tied up until the judge removes the order.

Inventory your assets

When you divorce, you're dividing your assets, so you need to know what those assets are. You must make an inventory of your possessions. You can walk around the house with a video camera, or just shoot a few rolls of film.

You also need to make copies of crucial financial records and store them in a safe place. This will help prevent disputes with your spouse if important records suddenly become "lost." Be sure to include statements from every bank, brokerage, savings, or other financial institution.

66 You are at risk any time you hold joint interest in, have responsibility with or are financially dependent upon your spouse or ex-spouse. You have no control over what may happen in the future should your former husband or wife default on payments, commit fraud, go bankrupt, die or become disabled and thereby jeopardize your financial position. *Violet Woodhouse & Victoria Collins with M.C. Blakeman, Divorce & Money* 99

Your spouse is hiding money

Hiding money during divorce is very common. If you think your spouse is hiding money, you have to look for *hidden income* or *concealed assets.*

Hidden income

If your spouse works for a large corporation, he may not be able to hide income because the corporation has to follow strict payroll laws. However, he may be able to defer bonuses or raises until the divorce is over.

But if your spouse is self-employed or has a small business, he has many opportunities to hide money by charging expenses to the business that lower his personal income.

If your spouse has his own business, look for the following warning signs:
- The business pays his personal expenses, such as his telephone bill, car, or meals.
- The business is cash-based.
- The business gave him a personal loan.
- The business has a high accounts receivable.
- He carries family members on the business payroll.
- He carries fictitious employees on the business payroll.

If you believe that your spouse is "cooking the books," you will have to do detailed *financial fact finding* to uncover the hidden money.

Concealed assets

To hide an asset, your spouse has to put it somewhere.

Physical assets—such as cars or boats—can be hidden in storage rooms. Stock certificates or bonds can be hidden in a private safe deposit box. And title to real property—such as a house—can be hidden by placing a phony name on the title.

Gather financial records

To find hidden money, you'll have to assemble financial records. Look for these:

Tax returns. You can get copies of tax returns by calling the IRS and requesting Form 4506. The IRS will send a copy to the address on the return. In addition to analyzing the return for suspicious deductions and expenses, look for unaccounted interest and dividends paid.

Bank and brokerage accounts. Not only will you have to examine every check that clears your joint accounts, but your spouse may have a secret account you know nothing about. If the account is under her name or uses her social security number, you'll have to hire a search firm to find the account.

Credit card receipts. You'll have the statements from your joint accounts, but if your spouse has an individual account, you will have to get a court order requiring him to turn these over. Examine the receipts to see where your spouse goes and what he spends his money on.

County records. If your spouse has any real property, there will be a record in the county recorder's office. Look for his name, the business name, and any other name he may use.

Insurance policies. If your spouse has an art, stamp, or coin collection you don't know about, she may have insured the collection. Check with every company you think she may do business with to see if there is an additional policy.

Loan applications. Finally, you can ask a court to make your spouse deliver copies of loan applications he has filled out with banks, brokerage houses, and credit unions. These documents will have a lot of information, and because they are signed by your spouse, they will be very useful in court.

Trace backwards

Once you've gathered this information—which may take a while—you still have to trace the transactions back to find the hidden money.

For example, if your spouse has received an unexplained interest payment, you'll have to find the asset that paid the interest. To do this, you'll need to hire a *forensic accountant,* an *actuary,* or a *business appraiser.*

❝ As cynical as it sounds, the temptation for your husband to try to cheat you out of your fair share of the marriage assets is almost always too great for him to resist. If there is some way he can defer income, conceal assets, flimflam you, he will probably do it. It usually requires a sainted man to resist the chance to deny you money or assets, and if he were such a sainted man, the chances are you wouldn't be getting a divorce. *Patricia Phillips, George Mair, Divorce: A Woman's Guide to Getting a Fair Share* ❞

107

You're overwhelmed with bills

When the divorce bills arrive in the mail, you may find it hard to stay afloat. Here's a strategy to help you cope with the "money crazies."

Make a budget

There's nothing magical about a budget. It doesn't help you lose weight or become younger. But it does help you spend less money.

To create a budget you need to do two things. You need to assemble a list of your expenses, and then decide how to pay those expenses. Here's how to do it:

Step 1. Write down everything you earn in a month.

Step 2. Write down everything you spend in a month by category. For example, rent, food, gas, and so on.

Step 3. Organize what you spend in order of importance. If you pay child support, put that high on your list because you must pay that.

Step 4. Cross-off or reduce those things at the bottom of your list. When you've crossed-off enough so that your income is more than your expenses—stop. You now have a balanced budget.

Step 5. On a sheet of paper, arrange two columns—the amount you can spend for each category, and a blank box. Then, *every day,* update that paper with how much you have spent. As you do this, you will see when you have spent too much in one category, and you have to "borrow" from another category to stay within your budget.

This may seem very simple—and it is—but knowing how you spend your money every month is all that a budget does. But it works. Try it!

Reduce your debts

If you want to reduce your debts, you have to examine your list to find ways to reduce your expenses. Do you spend $5 a day on lunch when you could spend $3? Can you find a cheaper calling plan and save $10 a month on your phone bill?

Once you have found some ways to squeeze out a few extra dollars a week, you can apply that money to repaying your debts. And if the debtor or credit card company is charging you more in interest than you can possibly repay, contact a consumer counseling service for help in negotiating your debt so you can eventually pay it off.

❝ If money is a problem for you, get your lawyer to assist you in finding a nonprofit consumer counseling service in your community that can help you. These advisers, such as the Consumer Credit Counseling Service, don't charge you for their services. *Melvin Belli, Divorcing* ❞

Your credit is bad

If you're behind in your bills, it will eventually hurt your credit. When that happens, the best thing to do is contact the major credit agencies.

Is your credit bad?

You know you're in trouble when:
- You're denied new credit.
- Creditors are contacting you.
- You can't pay the minimum amount due.
- You're using cash advances on one card to pay another.
- You don't know how much you owe.

If you are having problems, the first step is to look at your credit report.

Get your credit report

The three national credit reporting companies are Equifax, Trans Union, and Experian. Every time you buy something on credit and make a payment (or miss a payment), a record is sent to one of these companies where it is stored in your credit file.

You can see a copy of your file by writing a letter and asking for your credit report. If you have been turned down for credit within the last 30 days, you're entitled to a free copy.

Use the addresses in *Where to get help* to write to the credit agencies.

Once you've received your credit report, look it over for errors—either bad information that doesn't belong on your file, or good information that was left off your file.

Correct errors on your report

If there is an incorrect and harmful item on your credit report, write a letter to the credit agency and ask that it be removed. The agency has 30 days to check with the company that supplied the information. If it is not verified, it will be taken off your file.

But if the item is not removed, you can still send the credit agency a 100 word *statement of explanation* they must add to your file. Use this statement to explain why you disagree with the disputed item.

You can also write a letter to the credit agency if you have good credit they don't know about. In addition to the "big three" credit agencies, there are over 1,000 smaller agencies, and chances are, your credit file is incorrect or incomplete in many places.

66 Just because a debt is incurred after separation doesn't mean you won't get stuck paying your spouse's bills if it was charged on a joint account or credit card. Creditors may still come after you if your spouse defaults on payment, and your only recourse may be to pay the bill and try to get reimbursed from your ex-spouse. *Victoria Collins & Ginita Wall, Smart Ways to Save Money During & After Divorce* 99

You have to declare bankruptcy

When you are so deep in debt that there is no way you can repay it—you have to declare *bankruptcy*.

Bankruptcy is a legal way for you to wipe out most of your debts. Bankruptcy offers you a fresh start in life, a chance to avoid the mistakes that left you buried in debt in the first place.

That's the good news. The bad news is that bankruptcy severely damages your credit rating. After filing bankruptcy, you may be unable to borrow again for several years.

Types of bankruptcy

There are two types of bankruptcy for individuals. They are:

Chapter 7. Also called straight bankruptcy, this form of bankruptcy lets you wipe out—or discharge—most of your debts. Under Chapter 7, you may get to keep your house, but you'll probably have to sell other assets to pay your creditors. Also, certain debts, such as student loans, child support, and taxes, cannot be discharged.

Chapter 13. This form of bankruptcy does not immediately discharge your debts. Instead, you submit a plan to repay your creditors in 3 to 5 years. You can keep all your property, and your creditors must accept what you send them as payment in full, even if you don't pay back everything.

What happens in bankruptcy

Generally, your *unsecured* debts are wiped out in a bankruptcy. An unsecured debt is any debt not pledged to a specific piece of property. Examples of unsecured debts include:

- Credit cards
- Store charges
- Medical bills
- Legal bills
- Back utility bills
- Back rent

While many debts are discharged, certain types of debts are *nondischargeable*. This means that when the bankruptcy is over, you still owe the money. Examples include:

- Alimony
- Child support
- Student loans
- Federal, state, and local taxes
- Recent cash advances
- Recent charges for luxury items
- Debts you didn't list in the bankruptcy papers
- Debts incurred due to fraud, lying, or hiding assets

Calculate your debt-to-income ratio

To decide if bankruptcy is right for you, calculate your *debt-to-income ratio*. You do this by dividing your total dischargeable debts by your total income, and then multiplying by 100.

For example, if you have $40,000 in income and $12,000 in debts, you have a debt-to-income ration of 30%. But if you have $40,000 in income and $70,000 in debts, you have a debt-to-income ratio of 175% .

When bankruptcy makes sense

Bankruptcy makes sense when your ratio of dischargeable debts to income is over 50%. That is, if you owe more than 50% of what you earn, you may benefit from bankruptcy.

This rule-of-thumb is based on the fact that a chapter 7 bankruptcy will be erased from your credit report in 10 years. Thus, if it takes more than ten years to pay off your debts, you might as well wipe them out in bankruptcy.

How to file for bankruptcy

To declare bankruptcy, do the following:

1. File a bankruptcy petition in federal court. To locate the correct court, you have to find out which federal district you're in. Generally, the nearest large city has the court.

2. A bankruptcy trustee is appointed by the court. The trustee decides if you have enough property to pay back you creditors. If you don't, your bankruptcy proceeds.

3. The trustee sends a notice to your creditors informing them of your bankruptcy. At this time, the trustee sets a date for the meeting of the creditors.

4. You attend the meeting of the creditors. Don't be surprised if no one shows up. Generally, you'll just answer a few questions. You must go to this meeting.

5. You turn over to the trustee any non-exempt property. You can negotiate with the trustee on how to do this. For example, you can agree to hand over the property, or pay for it, or swap exempt property for nonexempt property.

6. You turn over to your creditors any collateral you have. You don't have any leeway on this since they have a legal right to repossess the property anyway.

7. You are granted your discharge. These court papers release you from any debts listed in your filing.

By the way, it costs you money to go bankrupt! The current filing fee for a Chapter 7 bankruptcy is $130, plus a $30 administrative fee. And that's the minimum. A bankruptcy lawyer will charge you as much as $1,000.

When bankruptcy doesn't make sense

If bankruptcy doesn't make sense, then consider asking your creditors for a loan *extension* or a loan *revision* until you can get back on your feet. You may be able to lower your monthly payments by extending the loan.

Or you may be able to get a consolidation loan that lowers your monthly payments. Or you may be able to sell off some personal property and use the money to pay your bills.

   " In days not so long gone, going into bankruptcy was a disgrace. Now it is a very common business strategy to stall creditors, reorganize your financial existence, and protect the businessman from financial pressures. So if your husband does that, don't pull out the hankie to wipe away your tears of sympathy. Call your lawyer instead and get a good accountant to confirm the truth about your husband's business or personal financial condition. *Patricia Phillips, George Mair, Divorce: A Woman's Guide to Getting a Fair Share* "

115

You can't afford a lawyer

If your divorce is simple, you may not need a lawyer. But nothing in court is ever *that* easy, and if you need legal help and you can't afford it, you have some alternatives.

Legal aid

To give everyone access to the law, the federal government created a business called the Legal Services Corporation—also called *legal aid.* The lawyers who work for legal aid help people who can't afford a lawyer.

To find out if you can get a legal aid lawyer, contact your local office and ask for help. Legal aid only accepts people who have very little money.

To find the nearest office, look in the phone book or call:

202-336-8800

This is the Washington, D.C. office. The operator can tell you where you can find a local office.

Pro bono programs

Another way to get free or inexpensive legal help is to use a volunteer lawyer. In every state, lawyers volunteer their time to help people who can't afford them.

To qualify for a *pro bono publico,* or "for the public good" program, your income must be low, and you must be able to prove it. Generally, you must earn less than $8,000 per year.

To find a program, call some local law firms and ask if they know about a pro bono program. You can also call your state bar and ask for information. The number for every state bar is in *State information.*

Self-help law books

A final alternative is to buy a book that has the forms you need and tells you how to file them with the court.

Many self-help books are available, with the best known coming from *Nolo Press.* They publish excellent divorce books, including books that help you do your own divorce, create a child custody plan, and modify child support. All of their books can be ordered from their website: *www.nolo.com*

If you use a self-help law book, be aware that each court has it's own rules, and your book may not have the specific rules you need. You can find out exactly what you need by hiring a paralegal or going to the court and asking the court clerk.

66 Doing your own divorce means that you take responsibility for your case, your decisions, your life. You get information and advice, then—perhaps with help—you think things through completely. You find out what the rules and legal standards are, how they apply to your case, then decide what you want, what's fair, how to deal with your spouse, what to do next. *Ed Sherman, How to Do Your Own Divorce in California* 99

You need child support

If you have children and are getting a divorce, you may be entitled to receive *child support.*

What is child support?

Child support is the money one parent pays the other to help raise the children.

Generally, the parent who has custody of the children—the *custodial* parent—receives money from the parent who does not have custody of the children—the *noncustodial* parent.

While both parents have a responsibility to support their children, the noncustodial parent meets his obligation by paying child support.

Types of child support

When you first get divorced, the judge may order *temporary* child support. This will last until the divorce is over, when the judge will order *permanent* child support.

It's important to know that child support has no effect on your taxes. The paying parent does not get a tax deduction, and the receiving parent does not report it as income.

That's why some parents combine child support with other payments—such as alimony—and call it *family* support. For you to get the tax breaks from this kind of arrangement, you must review it with both a divorce lawyer and a tax advisor.

How to get a child support order

You can always reach an agreement with your spouse about child support. But if you do not agree, you have to go to court. Here's how to do it:

1. Go to court and ask for the papers to get child support.

2. Fill out the papers and turn them into the court. You will be told the day you have to return for your *hearing*. You will also have to give a copy of the papers to your spouse.

3. Go to court for your hearing. At the hearing, tell the judge how much child support you need.

4. If the judge orders that you should receive child support, send a copy of the court order to your spouse's employer. In many states, the support will automatically be deducted from your spouse's paycheck and sent to you.

If you have some additional needs, you can ask the judge to include them in the support order. Examples of additional elements in a child support order include:
- Automatic cost of living adjustments to the support.
- Late payment fees if the support isn't paid on time.
- Security deposit if the support isn't paid at all.

Calculating child support

When the judge listens to you ask for support, he will use a mathematical formula or a table to calculate the correct amount to be paid. This is known as the *guideline* amount.

The guideline amount is based on several things, including how many children you have, how much money you earn,

119

and how much money your spouse earns. In some states, it includes how much time the children spend with your spouse.

Here's an example of a child support guideline table:

Children	Noncustodial parent's gross income
1	20%
2	25%
3	32%
4	37%
5+	42%

Awarding additional child support

Generally, the judge cannot give you less than the guideline amount, but he can give you more if you convince him that your children need more money for such things as:
- Medical expenses.
- Special education costs.
- Day care costs.
- Insurance costs.
- Hardship (if you've suffered a catastrophic loss).
- Travel costs (if you have to pay an unusual amount to bring your children to the other parent).

If you want the judge to give you more support, at your hearing, bring proof you need it for your children.

66 A child support order can always be modified if it is in the best interests of the child. However, guidelines were developed so there would be an efficient, predictable, standard method of calculating child support. *Beverly Pekala, Don't Settle for Less: A Woman's Guide to Getting a Fair Divorce & Custody Settlement* 99

You're not receiving your child support

If you're entitled to receive child support and you're not getting your money, you have to *enforce* the court order.

Enforcing a support order can be easy or difficult—it all depends on how much your spouse doesn't want to pay you. There are many tools available to help you, but it's up to you to use them.

Find your spouse

If your spouse has "disappeared," you need to find him. To find a missing parent, call your state *Child Support Enforcement Agency (CSE)*. The phone number for every support agency is in *State information.*

The CSE will use the *parent locator service* to find your missing spouse. This service searches through a variety of government databases, including:
• Social Security Administration.
• Department of Motor Vehicles.
• Department of Corrections.
• Internal Revenue Service.
• Veterans Administration.

Because it's almost impossible to exist without leaving some kind of a paper trail, the parent locator service is very successful. The *Office of Child Support Enforcement* reports a 70-80% success rate in finding missing parents.

Once you've found your spouse, you then have to enforce the court order.

Enforce the support order

The CSE can also help you collect your support. Ask the staff member assigned to your case to help you get your money. She can help you in many ways, including:

Wage Assignments. If your spouse is steadily employed or has a source of regular income, your support can be automatically deducted from his paycheck and sent to you.

Diversion of Government Benefits. Your support can also be taken out his unemployment compensation, worker's compensation, V.A. benefits, or other government benefits.

Property Liens. If your spouse owes back support, the CSE can help you place a lien on his property. A lien is a claim that gives you the right to be paid when the property is sold. The lien is not an actual source of cash, but rather, it's an order preventing the owner from selling, transferring, or borrowing against the property until the debt is paid.

Tax Refund Diversion. If your spouse owes back support and is expecting a tax refund, you can divert his refund to you. The state tax agency or IRS sends his refund to the child support agency, who then sends it to you.

IRS Full Collection Service. If your spouse owes a lot of back support, you can also use the IRS Full Collection Service to seize his property, attach his assets, and close his business.

Posting Bonds or Depositing Funds. Another way to collect support is to require that your spouse post a bond or deposit

122

funds into a security account. Then, if he falls behind in his payments, you can withdraw from the fund and he has to replenish it. The CSE can help you get the court order.

License Blocking. In some states, if your spouse owes child support, the state can block or revoke his driver's license, business license, or professional license.

Civil Contempt. If your spouse owes back support, the CSE attorney can request a *contempt of court* hearing. At the hearing, the judge will order your spouse to explain why the support is past due. If he was able to pay but chose not to, the judge can punish him. Contempt is serious, and the judge can do many things, including putting your spouse in jail.

Report to Credit Bureaus. Finally, you can ask the child support agency to report your spouse to the credit bureaus. This will limit his ability to borrow money until you get paid.

" A date of birth and a Social Security number are the most important nuggets of information you need to locate your ex-spouse. Usually, you'll remember his birthday, but rarely do you need instant knowledge of his Social Security number. Yet it can be found in some obvious, yet often overlooked, places. Joint bank account records, old insurance policies, hospital records, credit cards, and pay slips will contain his Social Security number. *Carl Hoffman, Deadbeat Dads: How to Find Them and Make Them Pay* "

You're behind in paying child support

When you get divorced, you're basically taking a private dispute to court.

But one part of divorce that is not private is the failure to pay child support. The law makes nonpayment of child support a *criminal offense.* And because it is a crime, the punishment is very serious.

If you cannot pay your child support, you must go to court and ask the judge to change the court order.

Go to court

Only a court can order you to pay child support, and only a court can change an existing support order. If you are ordered to pay child support and you cannot make the payments, you must go back to court and file a *motion* asking the judge to change the amount.

In your motion, you tell the judge what has changed since the last support order was made and why he must change the payments. If you lost your job or had to take lower pay—tell the judge.

Do not wait

It is very important that you do not wait before going back to court. Generally, a support order cannot be changed retroactively. If you get behind in your payments, the judge cannot "wipe out" what you owe. All he can do—if he's willing to do anything—is change how much you must pay from the day you filed your motion.

In some states, child support debts continue beyond when your children turn 18. Some states even allow a parent to pursue a child support debt for 10 years after the children reach adulthood.

Reluctant judges

More people return to court to modify child support than for any other reason. It's difficult to get a busy judge to change a support order, so be prepared to work very hard to convince the judge to do what you want.

The district attorney

Failure to pay child support is a crime, and if you get behind, the District Attorney can charge you with a crime. And if you are found guilty, you can go to jail.

That is why you must take child support very seriously. If there is a problem—go to court and tell the judge.

❝ Most domestic relations courts are extremely vigilant in protecting the support rights of children. In fact, many family court judges believe that their court's most important function is to ensure that child support is sufficient, appropriate and consistent within the law. *Jeffery Leving, Kenneth Dachman, Fathers' Rights* ❞

Where to get help

Equifax Credit Information Services
P.O. Box 105518
Atlanta, GA 30348
800-882-0648

Trans Union Consumer Relations
1561 E. Orangethorpe Ave.
Fullerton, CA 92831
800-916-8800

Experian
701 Experian Pkwy
Allen, TX 75013
888-397-3742

Consumer Credit Counseling Services
800-388-2227
Find out about counseling services in your area.

Internal Revenue Service
800-829-3676
Call for free tax forms and copies of your old returns.

Office of Child Support Enforcement
202-401-9373
This federal agency will direct you to a state agency that will
help you establish and collect a child support order.

Association for Children and Enforcement of Support
800-537-7072
A solid organization that helps with support enforcement.

More reading

Here are some helpful books on the money side of divorce. Be sure to check out *Divorce and Money* from Nolo Press. It's a well-researched book.

Child Support Survival Guide, Bonnie M. White, Douglas Pipes, Career Press, $12.99. An practical guide to understanding how child support works and how to deal with the federal Child Support Enforcement (CSE) agencies.

Deadbeat Dads: How to Find Them and Make Them Pay, Carl Hoffman, Pocket Books, 1996. A handy guide to finding a "missing" spouse.

Divorce and Money, Violet Woodhouse, Victoria F. Collins, Robin Leonard, M.C. Blakeman, Nolo Press, $26.95. This excellent book includes extremely detailed discussions of marital property, retirement benefits, insurance, taxes, business assets, debts, and spousal and child support.

Divorce: A Woman's Guide to Getting a Fair Share, Patricia Phillips, George Mair, Macmillan, 1995. Advice on the "divorce treasure hunt" from a family law attorney.

The Dollars and Sense of Divorce, Judith Briles, Carol Ann Wilson, Dearborn Financial Publishing, $17.95. An informative guide to dividing property, retirement plans, and so on. Includes a list of helpful organizations.

Don't Settle For Less, Beverly Pekala, Doubleday, $12.95. This book offers a step-by-step explanation for how women can avoid being economically victimized by divorce.

How to Collect Child Support, Geraldine Jensen with Katina Z. Jones, The Association for Children for Enforcement of Support, (ACES), Longmeadow Press, $7.95. An accurate and easy-to-follow guide to enforcing support orders.

How to File For Bankruptcy, Stephen Elias, Albin Renauer, and Robin Leonard, Nolo Press, 1994, $25.95. This book contains all of the forms and court addresses you need, plus an enormous amount of additional information.

The Single Parent's Money Guide, Emily W. Card, Macmillan, $14.95. Written by a lawyer, this book explains alimony and child support, insurance coverage, budgeting for medical emergencies, and other financial decisions.

Smart Ways to Save Money During & After Divorce, Victoria Collins & Ginita Wall, Nolo Press, 1994. 70 helpful tips to go through a divorce without going broke.

When Your Ex Won't Pay, Nancy S. Palmer and Ana Tangel-Rodriguez, Pinon Press, $12.00. Co-written by the Chair of the Florida Family Law Bar, this book explains the laws and various methods for collecting support.

State information

Alabama

Your child is missing...	**800-228-7688**
Your child is being hurt...	**800-422-4453**
You need to find a parent...	**205-242-9300**
You need to talk to someone...	**205-833-8336**

Child Support

Child Support Enforcement
Dept. of Human Resources
50 Ripley Street
Montgomery, AL 36130
205-242-9300

Domestic Violence

Alabama Coalition Against
Domestic Violence
P.O. Box 4762
Montgomery, AL 36101
334-832-4842

Alabama Coalition Against Rape
P.O. Box 4091
Montgomery, AL 36102
334-286-5980

State Police

Alabama Dept. of Public Safety
P.O. Box 1511
Montgomery, AL 36192

State Bar

Alabama State Bar
415 Dexter St.
Montgomery, AL 36104
205-269-1515

Alaska

Your child is missing...	**800-478-9333**
Your child is being hurt...	**800-478-4444**
You need to find a parent...	**907-263-6280**
You need to talk to someone...	**907-277-1300**

Child Support

Child Support Enforcement
Department of Revenue
550 West 7th Avenue
4th Floor
Anchorage, AK 99501
907-276-3441

Domestic Violence

Alaska Network on Domestic
Violence and Sexual Assault
130 Seward Street
Room 209
Juneau, AK 99801
907-586-3650

State Police

Alaska Dept. of Public Safety
P.O. Box N
Juneau, AK 99811

State Bar

Alaska Bar Association
510 L St. #602
Anchorage, AK 99501
907-272-7469

Arizona

Your child is missing...	**602-223-2158**
Your child is being hurt...	**888-767-2445**
You need to find a parent...	**602-252-4045**
You need to talk to someone...	**602-244-8166**

Child Support

Child Support Enforcement
Dept. of Economic Security
2222 W. Encanto
Phoenix, AZ 85067
602-252-0236

Domestic Violence

Arizona Coalition Against
Domestic Violence
100 West Camelback Road
Suite 109
Phoenix, AZ 85013
602-279-2900

State Police

Arizona Dept. of Public Safety
2102 W. Encino Blvd.
Phoenix, AZ 85005

State Bar

State Bar of Arizona
111 W. Monroe St.
Phoenix, AZ 85003
602-252-4804

Arkansas

Your child is missing...   **800-448-3014**

Your child is being hurt...   **800-482-5964**

You need to find a parent...   **501-252-8178**

You need to talk to someone...   **501-661-1548**

Child Support

Child Support Enforcement
Arkansas Social Services
P.O. Box 3358
Little Rock, AR 72203
501-682-8398

Domestic Violence

Arkansas Coalition Against
Domestic Violence
#1 Sheriff Lane
Suite C
North Little Rock, AR 72114
501-812-0571

Arkansas Coalition Against
Violence to Women and
Children
523 Louisiana
Suite 230
Little Rock, AR 72201
800-269-4668

State Police

Arkansas Dept. of Public Safety
Three Natural Resources Dr.
Little Rock, AR 72215

State Bar

Arkansas Bar Association
400 W. Markham
Little Rock, AR 72201
501-375-4605

California

Your child is missing...   **800-222-3463**

Your child is being hurt...   **800-422-4453**

You need to find a parent...   **916-227-3600**

You need to talk to someone...   **916-567-0163**

Child Support

Child Support Program
Management Branch
Dept. of Social Services
744 P Street
Sacramento, CA 95814
916-323-8994

Domestic Violence

Coalition to End Domestic and
Sexual Violence
2064 Eastman Ave.
Suite 104
Ventura, CA 93003
805-656-1111

California Coalition Against
Sexual Assault Rape Prevention
Resource Center
1611 Telegraph Avenue
Suite 1515
Oakland, CA 94612
510-839-8825

State Police

California State Dept. of Justice
P.O. Box 944255
Sacramento, CA 94244

State Bar

State Bar of California
555 Franklin St.
San Francisco, CA 94102
415-561-8200

Colorado

Your child is missing...	**303-239-4222**
Your child is being hurt...	**800-422-4453**
You need to find a parent...	**303-866-3353**
You need to talk to someone...	**303-321-3104**

Child Support

Child Support Enforcement
Dept. of Social Services
1575 Sherman St.
Denver, CO 80203
303-866-5994

Domestic Violence

Colorado Domestic Violence
Coalition
P.O. Box 18902
Denver, CO 80218
888-778-7091

Colorado Coalition Against
Sexual Assault
P.O. Box 18663
Denver, CO 80218
303-861-7033

State Police

Colorado Bureau of
Investigation
690 Kipling St.
Lakewood, CO 80215

State Bar

The Colorado Bar Association
1900 Grant St.
#950
Denver, CO 80203
303-860-1115

Connecticut

Your child is missing...   **203-238-6575**

Your child is being hurt...   **800-842-2288**

You need to find a parent...   **203-566-5438**

You need to talk to someone...   **860-586-2319**

Child Support

Child Support Enforcement
Dept of Human Resources
1049 Asylum Avenue
Hartford, CT 06105
203-566-3053

Domestic Violence

Connecticut Sexual Assault
Crisis Services, Inc.
110 Connecticut Blvd.
East Hartford, CT 06108
860-282-9881

State Police

Connecticut State Police
Department
294 Colony St.
Meriden, CT 06450

State Bar

Connecticut State Bar
Association
101 Corporate Place
Rocky Hill, CT 06067
203-721-0025

Delaware

Your child is missing...   **302-739-5883**

Your child is being hurt...   **800-292-9582**

You need to find a parent...   **302-577-4832**

You need to talk to someone...   **302-427-0787**

Child Support

Child Support Enforcement
Dept. of Health & Social
Services
P.O. Box 904
New Castle, DE 19720
302-421-8300

Domestic Violence

Delaware Coalition Against
Domestic Violence
P.O. Box 847
Wilmington, DE 19899
302-658-2958

State Police

Delaware State Police Dept.
P.O. Box 430
Dover, DE 19903

State Bar

Delaware State Bar Association
1225 King Street
Wilmington, DE 19801
302-658-5279

District of Columbia

Your child is missing...   **202-576-6771**

Your child is being hurt...   **800-422-4453**

You need to find a parent...   **202-727-5046**

You need to talk to someone...   **202-546-0646**

Child Support

Office of Paternity & Child
Support
Dept. of Human Services
425 I Street, NW
Washington, DC 20001
202-724-5610

Domestic Violence

D.C. Coalition Against Domestic
Violence
513 U Street NW
Washington, DC 20001
202-783-5332

State Police

Dept. of Public Safety
P.O. Box 1606
Washington, DC 20013

State Bar

Bar Association of the District of
Columbia
1819 H Street, NW
Washington, DC 20006
202-223-6600

The District of Columbia Bar
1250 H Street, NW
Washington, DC 20005
202-737-4700

Florida

Your child is missing...   **800-342-0821**

Your child is being hurt...   **800-962-2873**

You need to find a parent...   **904-488-9907**

You need to talk to someone...   **877-626-4352**

Child Support

Child Support Enforcement
Dept. of Health & Rehabilitative
Services
1317 Winewood Blvd., Bldg-3
Tallahassee, FL 32399
904-488-9900

Domestic Violence

Florida Coalition Against
Domestic Violence
308 East Park Avenue
Tallahassee, FL 32301
800-500-1119

Florida Council of Sexual Abuse
Services, Inc.
410 Office Plaza Drive
Tallahassee, FL 32301
850-671-5150

State Police

Florida Department of Law
Enforcement
P.O. Box 1489
Tallahassee, FL 32302

State Bar

The Florida Bar
650 Apalachee Parkway
Tallahassee, FL 32399
904-561-5600

Georgia

Your child is missing...	**800-282-6564**
Your child is being hurt...	**800-422-4453**
You need to find a parent...	**404-894-5933**
You need to talk to someone...	**770-234-0855**

Child Support

Child Support Recovery
Dept. of Human Resources
878 Peach Tree N.E.
Room 529
Atlanta, GA 30309
404-894-4119

Domestic Violence

Georgia Advocates for Battered
Women and Children
250 Georgia Avenue, S.E.
Suite 308
Atlanta, GA 30312
800-643-1212

Georgia Rape Crisis Program
2762 Watson Blvd.
Warner Robins, GA 31093
912-953-5675

State Police

Department of State Police
P.O. Box 370748
Decatur, GA 30037

State Bar

State Bar of Georgia
50 Hurt Plaza
Atlanta, GA 30303
404-527-8700

Hawaii

Your child is missing...   **808-586-1416**

Your child is being hurt...   **800-422-4453**

You need to find a parent...   **808-587-3772**

You need to talk to someone... **808-591-1297**

Child Support

Child Support Enforcement
Dept. of the Attorney General
680 Iwilei Rd.
Suite 490
Honolulu, HI 96817
808-587-3712

Domestic Violence

Hawaii State Coalition Against
Domestic Violence
98-939 Moanalua Road
Aiea, HI 96701
808-486-5072

Hawaii State Coalition Against
Sexual Assault
1164 Bishop Street
Suite 124
Honolulu, HI 96813
808-595-0174

State Police

Hawaii Dept. of Public Safety
465 S. King St.
Honolulu, HI 96813

State Bar

Hawaii State Bar Association
1136 Union Mall
Honolulu, HI 96813
808-537-1868

141

Idaho

Your child is missing...   **800-843-5678**

Your child is being hurt...   **800-422-4453**

You need to find a parent...   **208-334-6670**

You need to talk to someone...   **208-673-6672**

Child Support

Child Support Enforcement
Dept. of Health & Welfare
450 W. State Street
Boise, ID 83720
208-334-5710

Domestic Violence

Idaho Coalition Against Sexual
and Domestic Violence
815 Park Blvd.
Suite 140
Boise, ID 83712
888-293-6118

State Police

Idaho Dept. of State Police
6083 Clinton St.
Boise, ID 83704

State Bar

Idaho State Bar
525 W Jefferson
Boise, ID 83701
208-334-4500

Illinois

Your child is missing...	**800-843-5763**
Your child is being hurt...	**800-252-2873**
You need to find a parent...	**217-524-4568**
You need to talk to someone...	**217-522-1403**

Child Support

Child Support Enforcement
Dept. of Public Aid
201 South Grand Ave. East
Springfield, IL 62794
217-782-1366

Domestic Violence

Illinois Coalition Against
Domestic Violence
801 South 11th Street
Springfield, IL 62703
217-789-2830

Illinois Coalition Against Sexual
Assault
123 S. 7th Street
Suite 500
Springfield, IL 62701
217-753-4117

State Police

Illinois Department of State
Police
260 N. Chicago St.
Joliet, IL 60431

State Bar

Illinois State Bar Association
424 S. Second St.
Springfield, IL 62701
217-525-1760

Indiana

Your child is missing...	**800-831-8953**
Your child is being hurt...	**800-562-2407**
You need to find a parent...	**317-232-4936**
You need to talk to someone...	**317-925-9399**

Child Support

Child Support Enforcement
Dept. of Public Welfare
402 West Washington St.
Room W360
Indianapolis, IN 46204
317-232-4885

Domestic Violence

Indiana Coalition Against
Domestic Violence
2511 E. 46th St.
Suite N-3
Indianapolis, IN 46205
800-332-7385

Indiana Coalition Against Sexual
Assault
2511 E. 46th St.
Suite N-3
Indianapolis, IN 46205
317-568-4001

State Police

Indiana State Police
100 N. Senate Ave.
Indianapolis, IN 46204

State Bar

Indiana State Bar Association
230 E. Ohio St.
4th Floor
Indianapolis, IN 46204
317-639-5465

Iowa

Your child is missing...   **800-346-5507**

Your child is being hurt...   **800-362-2178**

You need to find a parent...   **515-281-8970**

You need to talk to someone...   **515-254-0417**

Child Support

Bureau of Collections
Iowa Dept. of Human Services
Hoover Building
5th Floor
Des Moines, IA 50319
515-281-5580

Domestic Violence

Iowa Coalition Against Domestic
Violence
2603 Bell Ave.
Suite 100
Des Moines, IA 50321
800-942-0333

Iowa Coalition Against Sexual
Assault
2603 Bell St.
Suite 102
Des Moines, IA 50321
515-244-7424

State Police

Iowa Dept. of Public Safety
Wallace State Office Building
Des Moines, IA 50319

State Bar

The Iowa State Bar Association
521 E. Locust
Des Moines, IA 50309
515-243-3179

Kansas

Your child is missing...   **800-572-7463**

Your child is being hurt...   **800-922-5330**

You need to find a parent...   **913-296-1450**

You need to talk to someone...   **785-233-0755**

Child Support

Child Support Enforcement
Dept. of Social & Rehabilitation
Services
300 South West Oakley St.
Topeka, KS 66603
913-296-3237

Domestic Violence

Kansas Coalition Against Sexual
and Domestic Violence
820 S.E. Quincy
Suite 600
Topeka, KS 66612
785-232-9784

State Police

Kansas Bureau of Public Safety
1620 Southwest Tyler
Topeka, KS 66612

State Bar

Kansas Bar Association
1200 Harrison Street
Topeka, KS 66612
913-234-5696

Kentucky

Your child is missing...   **800-222-5555**

Your child is being hurt...   **800-752-6200**

You need to find a parent...   **502-564-2244**

You need to talk to someone...   **502-245-5284**

Child Support

Child Support Enforcement
Dept. of Social Insurance
275 East Main Street
6th Floor East
Frankfort, KY 40621
502-564-2285

Domestic Violence

Kentucky Domestic Violence
Association
P.O. Box 356
Frankfort, KY 40602
502-875-4132

Kentucky Association of Sexual
Assault Programs, Inc.
P.O. Box 602
Frankfort, KY 40602
502-226-2704

State Police

Kentucky State Police
1250 Louisville Rd.
Frankfort, KY 40601

State Bar

Kentucky Bar Association
514 West Main
Frankfort, KY 40601
502-564-3795

Louisiana

Your child is missing...	**504-342-4011**
Your child is being hurt...	**800-422-4453**
You need to find a parent...	**504-342-5131**
You need to talk to someone...	**225-343-6928**

Child Support

Support Enforcement Services
Dept. of Social Services
P.O. Box 94065
Baton Rouge, LA 70804
504-342-4780

Domestic Violence

Louisiana Coalition Against
Domestic Violence
P.O. Box 77308
Baton Rouge, LA 70879
225-752-1296

Louisiana Foundation Against
Sexual Assault
685 W. Railroad Ave.
Suite A
Independence, LA 70443
800-960-7273

State Police

Louisiana Dept. of Public Safety
P.O. Box 66614
Baton Rouge, LA 70896

State Bar

Louisiana State Bar Association
601 St. Charles Ave.
New Orleans, LA 70130
504-566-1600

Maine

Your child is missing...   **800-452-4664**

Your child is being hurt...   **800-452-1999**

You need to find a parent...   **202-401-9267**

You need to talk to someone...   **207-622-5767**

Child Support

Support Enforcement and
Recovery
Dept. of Human Services
State House
Station 11
Augusta, ME 04333
207-289-2886

Domestic Violence

Maine Coalition to End
Domestic Violence
128 Main Street
Bangor, ME 04401
207-941-1194

Maine Coalition Against Sexual
Assault
3 Milliken Court
Augusta, ME 04330
207-626-0034

State Police

Maine State Police
36 Hospital St.
Augusta, ME 04330

State Bar

Maine State Bar Association
124 State St.
Augusta, ME 04330
207-622-7523

Maryland

Your child is missing...   **800-637-5437**

Your child is being hurt...   **800-332-6347**

You need to find a parent...   **301-333-0635**

You need to talk to someone...   **410-467-7100**

Child Support

Child Support Enforcement
Dept. of Human Resources
311 W. Saratoga St.
Baltimore, MD 21201
401-333-3979

Domestic Violence

Maryland Network Against
Domestic Violence
6911 Laurel Bowie Rd.
Suite 309
Bowie, MD 20715
800-634-3577

Maryland Coalition Against
Sexual Assault
7257 Parkway Drive
Suite 208
Hanover, MD 21076
800-656-4673

State Police

Maryland State Police
1201 Reistertown Rd.
Pikesville, MD 21208

State Bar

Maryland State Bar Association
520 W. Fayette St.
Baltimore, MD 21201
410-685-7878

Massachusetts

Your child is missing...   **800-622-5999**

Your child is being hurt...   **800-792-5200**

You need to find a parent...   **207-289-2886**

You need to talk to someone...   **781-938-4048**

Child Support

Child Support Enforcement
Dept. of Revenue
141 Portland St.
Cambridge, MA 02139
617-621-4200

Domestic Violence

Massachusetts Coalition Against
Sexual Assault and Domestic
Violence
14 Beacon Street
Suite 507
Boston, MA 02108
617-248-0922

Massachusetts Coalition Against
Sexual Assault
146 West Boylston
Worcester, MA 01608
508-852-7600

State Police

Massachusetts Dept. of Public
Safety
One Ashburton Place
Boston, MA 02108

State Bar

Massachusetts Bar Association
20 West St.
Boston, MA 02111
617-542-3602

Michigan

Your child is missing...   **517-336-6603**

Your child is being hurt...   **800-942-4357**

You need to find a parent...   **517-373-8640**

You need to talk to someone...   **517-485-4049**

Child Support

Office of Child Support
Dept. of Social Services
235 Grand Avenue
Suite 1046
Lansing, MI 48909
517-373-7570

Domestic Violence

Bay County Women's Center
P.O. Box 1458
Bay City, MI 48706
517-265-6776

Michigan Coalition Against
Domestic & Sexual Violence
913 W. Homes
Suite 211
Lansing, MI 48910
517-887-9334

State Police

Michigan Dept. of State Police
714 S. Harrison Rd.
East Lansing, MI 48823

State Bar

State Bar of Michigan
306 Townsend St.
Lansing, MI 48933
517-372-9030

152

Minnesota

Your child is missing...   **612-642-0610**

Your child is being hurt...   **800-422-4453**

You need to find a parent...   **612-297-1113**

You need to talk to someone...   **651-645-2948**

Child Support

Child Support Enforcement
Dept. of Human Services
444 Lafayette
4th Floor
St. Paul, MN 55155
612-296-2499

Domestic Violence

Minnesota Coalition for
Battered Women
450 North Syndicate Street
Suite 122
St. Paul, MN 55104
651-646-0994

Minnesota Coalition Against
Sexual Assault
2344 Nicollett Ave. S.
#170A
Minneapolis, MN 55404
612-872-7734

State Police

Minnesota Dept. of Public
Safety
1246 University Ave.
St. Paul, MN 55104

State Bar

Minnesota State Bar
Association
514 Nicollet Mall
Suite 300
Minneapolis, MN 55402
612-333-1183

153

Mississippi

Your child is missing...   601-987-1592

Your child is being hurt...   800-222-8000

You need to find a parent...   601-354-6845

You need to talk to someone...   601-981-4491

Child Support

Child Support Division
Dept. of Human Services
515 E. Amite Street
Jackson, MS 39205
601-354-0341

Domestic Violence

Mississippi State Coalition
Against Domestic Violence
P.O. Box 4703
Jackson, MS 39296
800-898-3234

Mississippi Coalition Against
Sexual Assault
5455 Executive Place Drive
Jackson, MS 39296
601-987-9011

State Police

Mississippi Dept. of Public
Safety
P.O. Box 958
Jackson, MS 39205

State Bar

Mississippi State Bar
643 N State Street
Jackson, MS 39202
601-948-4471

Missouri

Your child is missing...   **800-877-3452**

Your child is being hurt...   **800-392-3738**

You need to find a parent...   **314-751-2464**

You need to talk to someone...   **573-634-7727**

Child Support

Child Support Enforcement
Dept. of Social Services
P.O. Box 1527
Jefferson City, MO 65102
314-751-4301

Domestic Violence

Missouri Coalition Against
Domestic Violence
415 E. McCarty Street
Jefferson City, MO 65101
573-634-4161

Missouri Coalition Against
Sexual Assault
P.O. Box 16771
St. Louis, MO 63105
816-931-4527

State Police

Missouri Dept. of Public Safety
1510 E. Elm St.
Jefferson City, MO 65102

State Bar

The Missouri Bar
326 Monroe
Jefferson City, MO 65102
314-635-4128

Montana

Your child is missing...   **800-332-6617**

Your child is being hurt...   **800-332-6100**

You need to find a parent...   **406-657-6101**

You need to talk to someone... **406-443-7871**

Child Support

Child Support Enforcement
Dept. of Social & Rehabilitation
Services
P.O. Box 5955
Helena, MT 59604
406-444-4614

Domestic Violence

Montana Coalition Against
Domestic and Sexual Violence
P.O. Box 633
Helena, MT 59624
406-443-7794

State Police

Montana Dept. of State Police
303 N. Roberts
Helena, MT 59620

State Bar

State Bar of Montana
46 North Last Chance Gulch
Helena, MT 59624
406-442-7660

Nebraska

Your child is missing...   **402-479-4019**

Your child is being hurt...   **800-652-1999**

You need to find a parent...   **402-471-9349**

You need to talk to someone... **877-463-6264**

Child Support

Child Support Enforcement
Dept. of Social Services
P.O. Box 95026
Lincoln, NE 68509
402-471-9125

Domestic Violence

Nebraska Domestic Violence
and Sexual Assault Coalition
825 M Street
Suite 404
Lincoln, NE 68508
800-876-6238

State Police

Nebraska State Police
P.O. Box 94907
Lincoln, NE 68509

State Bar

Nebraska State Bar Association
635 S. 14th Street
2nd Floor
Lincoln, NE 68508
402-475-7091

Nevada

Your child is missing...   **702-486-3420**

Your child is being hurt...   **800-992-5757**

You need to find a parent...   **702-687-4960**

You need to talk to someone...   **702-258-1618**

Child Support

Child Support Enforcement
Dept. of Human Resources
2527 N. Carson Street
Carson City, NV 89710
702-885-4744

Domestic Violence

Nevada Network Against
Domestic Violence
100 West Grove
Suite 315
Reno, NV 89509
800-500-1556

State Police

Nevada Dept. of Public Safety
555 Wright Way
Carson City, NV 89711

State Bar

State Bar of Nevada
201 Las Vegas Blvd.
Suite 200
Las Vegas, NV 89101
702-382-2200

New Hampshire

Your child is missing...   **800-852-3411**

Your child is being hurt...   **800-894-5533**

You need to find a parent...   **603-271-4422**

You need to talk to someone...   **603-225-5359**

Child Support

Child Support Enforcement
Division of Human Services
6 Hazen Drive
Concord, NH 03301
603-271-4426

Domestic Violence

New Hampshire Coalition
Against Domestic and Sexual
Violence
P.O. Box 353
Concord, NH 03302
800-852-3388

State Police

New Hampshire State Police
10 Hazen Dr.
Concord, NH 03305

State Bar

New Hampshire Bar Association
112 Pleasant St.
Concord, NH 03301
603-224-6942

New Jersey

Your child is missing...   **800-743-5377**

Your child is being hurt...   **800-792-8610**

You need to find a parent...   **609-588-2355**

You need to talk to someone... **732- 940-0991**

Child Support

Department of Human Services
Bureau of Child Support and
Paternity Programs
CN 716
Trenton, NJ 08625
609-588-2361

Domestic Violence

New Jersey Coalition for
Battered Women
2620 Whitehorse/Hamilton
Square Road
Trenton, NJ 08690
609-584-8107

New Jersey Coalition Against
Sexual Assault
One Roosevelt Drive
Edison, NJ 08837
908-418-1354

State Police

New Jersey State Police
P.O. Box 7068
West Trenton, NJ 08628

State Bar

New Jersey State Bar
Association
One Constitution Square
New Brunswick, NJ 08901
908-249-5000

160

New Mexico

Your child is missing...   **505-827-9187**

Your child is being hurt...   **800-432-2075**

You need to find a parent...   **505-827-7221**

You need to talk to someone...   **505-260-0154**

Child Support

Child Support Enforcement
Dept. of Human Services
P.O. Box 25109
Santa Fe, NM 87504
505-827-7200

Domestic Violence

New Mexico State Coalition
Against Domestic Violence
P.O. Box 25266
Albuquerque, NM 87125
800-773-3645

New Mexico Coalition of Sexual
Assault Programs, Inc.
4004 Carlisle, NE
Suite D
Albuquerque, NM 87107
505-883-8020

State Police

New Mexico Dept. of Public
Safety
P.O. Box 1628
Santa Fe, NM 87504

State Bar

State Bar of New Mexico
P.O. Box 25883
Albuquerque, NM 87125
505-842-6132

New York

Your child is missing...	**800-346-3543**
Your child is being hurt...	**800-342-3720**
You need to find a parent...	**518-474-9092**
You need to talk to someone...	**518-462-2000**

Child Support

Child Support Enforcement
New York State Dept. of Social
Services
1 Commerce Plaza
Albany, NY 12260
518-474-9081

Domestic Violence

New York State Coalition
Against Domestic Violence
79 Central Avenue
Albany, NY 12206
800-942-6906

New York State Coalition
Against Sexual Assault
79 Central Avenue
Albany, NY 12206
518-434-4580

State Police

New York State Police
Executive Park Tower
Albany, NY 12203

State Bar

New York State Bar Association
One Elk St.
Albany, NY 12207
518-463-3200

North Carolina

Your child is missing...	**800-522-5437**
Your child is being hurt...	**800-422-4453**
You need to find a parent...	**919-571-4120**
You need to talk to someone...	**919-788-0801**

Child Support

Child Support Enforcement
Dept. of Social Services
100 East Six Forks Rd.
Raleigh, NC 27609
919-571-4120

Domestic Violence

North Carolina Coalition Against
Domestic Violence
301 W. Main Street
Durham, NC 27701
919-956-9124

North Carolina Coalition Against
Sexual Assault
174 Mine Lake Court
Suite 1000
Raleigh, NC 27615
919-676-7611

State Police

North Carolina Dept. of Public
Safety
407 Blount St.
Raleigh, NC 27602

State Bar

North Carolina State Bar
208 Fayetteville Street Mall
Raleigh, NC 27611
919-828-4620

North Carolina Bar Association
1312 Annapolis Drive
Raleigh, NC 27608
919-828-0561

North Dakota

Your child is missing...   **800-472-2121**

Your child is being hurt...   **800-422-4453**

You need to find a parent...   **701-224-5486**

You need to talk to someone...   **701-838-6501**

Child Support

Child Support Enforcement
Dept. of Human Services
P.O. Box 7190
Bismarck, ND 58507
701-224-3582

Domestic Violence

North Dakota Council on Abused
Women's Services
418 East Rosser Ave.
Suite 320
Bismarck, ND 58501
800-472-2911

State Police

North Dakota Bureau of
Investigations
P.O. Box 1054
Bismarck, ND 58502

State Bar

State Bar Association of North
Dakota
515-1/2 E. Broadway
Suite 101
Bismarck, ND 58502
701-255-1404

Ohio

Your child is missing...   **800-325-5604**

Your child is being hurt...   **800-422-4453**

You need to find a parent...   **614-752-6567**

You need to talk to someone...   **614-224-2700**

Child Support

Bureau of Child Support
Ohio Dept. of Human Services
30 East Broad Street
Columbus, OH 43266
614-752-6561

Domestic Violence

Ohio Domestic Violence
Network
4041 North High Street
Suite 400
Columbus, OH 43214
800-934-9840

Ohio Coalition on Sexual Assault
4041 N. High Street
Suite 408
Columbus, OH 43214
614-268-3322

State Police

Ohio Dept. of Investigations
P.O. Box 365
London, OH 43140

State Bar

Ohio State Bar Association
1700 Lake Shore Drive
Columbus, OH 43216
614-487-2050

Oklahoma

Your child is missing...   **405-848-6724**

Your child is being hurt...   **800-522-3511**

You need to find a parent...   **405-424-5871**

You need to talk to someone...   **405-848-4330**

Child Support

Child Support Enforcement
Dept. of Human Services
P.O. Box 25352
Oklahoma City, OK 73125
405-424-5871

Domestic Violence

Oklahoma Coalition Against
Domestic Violence and Sexual
Assault
2525 NW Expressway
Suite 208
Oklahoma City, OK 73116
800-522-9054

State Police

Oklahoma Dept. of Public Safety
P.O. Box 11497
Oklahoma City, OK 73136

State Bar

Oklahoma Bar Association
1901 N. Lincoln
Oklahoma City, OK 73105
405-524-2365

Oregon

Your child is missing...	**503-378-3720**
Your child is being hurt...	**800-854-3508**
You need to find a parent...	**503-373-7300**
You need to talk to someone...	**503-370-7774**

Child Support

Adult and Family Services
Division
Dept. of Human Resources
P.O. Box 14506
Salem, OR 97309
503-378-5439

Domestic Violence

Oregon Coalition Against
Domestic and Sexual Violence
520 N.W. Davis
Suite 310
Portland, OR 97209
800-622-3782

State Police

Oregon State Police
3772 Portland Rd.
Salem, OR 97310

State Bar

Oregon State Bar
P.O. Box 1689
Lake Oswego, OR 97035
503-620-0222

Pennsylvania

Your child is missing...	**717-783-5524**
Your child is being hurt...	**800-932-0313**
You need to find a parent...	**717-783-3032**
You need to talk to someone...	**717-238-1514**

Child Support

Child Support Enforcement
Dept. of Public Welfare
P.O. Box 8018
Harrisburg, PA 17105
717-783-3672

Domestic Violence

Pennsylvania Coalition Against
Domestic Violence
6440 Flank Dr.
Suite 1300
Harrisburg, PA 17112
800-932-4632

Pennsylvania Coalition Against
Rape
125 Enola Drive
Enola, PA 17025
800-692-7445

State Police

Pennsylvania State Police
1800 Elmerton Ave.
Harrisburg, PA 17110

State Bar

Pennsylvania Bar Association
100 South Street
Harrisburg, PA 17108
717-238-6715

Rhode Island

Your child is missing...   **800-286-8626**

Your child is being hurt...   **800-742-4453**

You need to find a parent...   **401-464-3014**

You need to talk to someone...   **401-331-3060**

Child Support

Bureau of Family Support
Dept. of Human Services
77 Dorance Street
Providence, RI 02903
401-277-2409

Domestic Violence

Rhode Island Coalition Against
Domestic Violence
422 Post Rd.
Suite 202
Warwick, RI 02888
800-494-8100

State Police

Rhode Island Dept. of Public
Safety
72 Pine St.
Providence, RI 02903

State Bar

Rhode Island Bar Association
115 Cedar Street
Providence, RI 02903
401-421-5740

South Carolina

Your child is missing...   **800-322-4453**

Your child is being hurt...   **800-422-4453**

You need to find a parent...   **803-737-5820**

You need to talk to someone...   **803-754-4447**

Child Support

Child Support Enforcement
Dept. of Social Services
P.O. Box 1520
Columbia, SC 29202
803-737-9938

Domestic Violence

South Carolina Coalition Against
Domestic Violence & Sexual
Assault
P.O. Box 7776
Columbia, SC 29202
800-260-9293

State Police

South Carolina Dept. of Law
Enforcement
P.O. Box 21398
Columbia, SC 29221

State Bar

South Carolina Bar Association
950 Taylor Street
Columbia, SC 29202
803-799-6653

South Dakota

Your child is missing...   **605-773-3331**

Your child is being hurt...   **800-422-4453**

You need to find a parent...   **605-773-5189**

You need to talk to someone...   **605-697-7210**

Child Support

Child Support Enforcement
Dept. of Social Services
700 Governors Drive
Pierre, SD 57501
605-773-3641

Domestic Violence

South Dakota Coalition Against
Domestic Violence and Sexual
Assault
P.O. Box 141
Pierre, SD 57501
800-572-9196

State Police

South Dakota Division of
Criminal Investigation
500 E. Capitol Ave.
Pierre, SD 57501

State Bar

State Bar of South Dakota
222 E. Capitol
Pierre, SD 57501
605-224-7554

Tennessee

Your child is missing...   **615-741-0430**

Your child is being hurt...   **800-422-4453**

You need to find a parent...   **615-741-7923**

You need to talk to someone...   **865-602-7900**

Child Support

Child Support Services
Dept. of Human Services
400 Deadrick Street
Nashville, TN 37219
615-741-1820

Domestic Violence

Tennessee Task Force Against
Domestic Violence
P.O. Box 120972
Nashville, TN 37212
800-356-6767

Tennessee Coalition Against
Sexual Assault
P.O. Box 120972
Nashville, TN 37212
800-289-9018

State Police

Tennessee Dept. of Public
Safety
1150 Foster Ave.
Nashville, TN 37224

State Bar

Tennessee Bar Association
3622 West End Avenue
Nashville, TN 37205
615-383-7421

Texas

Your child is missing...   **800-346-3243**

Your child is being hurt...   **800-252-5400**

You need to find a parent...   **512-463-2181**

You need to talk to someone...   **512-374-9339**

Child Support

Child Support Enforcement
Office of the Attorney General
P.O. Box 12017
Austin, TX 78711
512-463-2181

Domestic Violence

Texas Council on Family
Violence
P.O. Box 161810
Austin, TX 78716
800-525-1978

Texas Association Against
Sexual Assault
800 Brazos
Suite 1040
Austin, TX 78701
512-474-8161

State Police

Texas State Police
P.O. Box 4143
Austin, TX 78765

State Bar

State Bar of Texas
1414 Colorado
Austin, TX 78701
800-204-2222

173

Utah

Your child is missing...	**800-843-5678**
Your child is being hurt...	**800-422-4453**
You need to find a parent...	**801-538-4677**
You need to talk to someone...	**801-323-9900**

Child Support

Office of Recovery Services
Dept. of Social Services
120 North 200 West
Salt Lake City, UT 84145
801-538-4400

Domestic Violence

Domestic Violence Advisory
Council
120 North 200 West
Salt Lake City, UT 84103
800-897-5465

CAUSE
366 South 500 East
Suite 212
Salt Lake City, UT 84102
801-322-5000

State Police

Utah Dept. of Public Safety
4501 S. 2700 West Ave.
Salt Lake City, UT 84119

State Bar

Utah State Bar
645 S. 200 East
#310
Salt Lake City, UT 84111
801-531-9077

Vermont

Your child is missing...   **802-773-9101**

Your child is being hurt...   **800-422-4453**

You need to find a parent...   **802-241-2891**

You need to talk to someone...   **802-244-1396**

Child Support

Child Support Division
Agency of Human Services
103 South Main Street
Waterbury, VT 05676
802-241-2319

Domestic Violence

Vermont Network Against
Domestic Violence and Sexual
Assault
P.O. Box 405
Montpelier, VT 05601
800-489-7273

State Police

Vermont State Police
103 S. Main St.
Waterbury, VT 05676

State Bar

Vermont Bar Association
35-37 Court Street
Montpelier, VT 05602
802-223-2020

175

Virginia

Your child is missing...   **800-822-4453**

Your child is being hurt...   **800-552-7096**

You need to find a parent...   **804-662-9627**

You need to talk to someone...   **804-225-8264**

Child Support

Child Support Enforcement
Dept. of Social Services
8007 Discovery Drive
Richmond, VA 23288
804-662-9629

Domestic Violence

Virginians Family Violence and
Sexual Assault Hotline
2850 Sandy Bay Road
Suite 101
Williamsburg, VA 23185
800-838-8238

Virginians Aligned Against
Sexual Assault
508 Dale Avenue
Charlottesville, VA 22903
804-979-9002

State Police

State Police of Virginia
P.O. Box 27272
Richmond, VA 23261

State Bar

Virginia State Bar
707 E. Main St.
Suite 1500
Richmond, VA 23219
804-775-0500

Virginia Bar Association
701 E. Franklin St.
#1515
Richmond, VA 23219
804-644-0041

Washington

Your child is missing...   **800-543-5678**

Your child is being hurt...   **800-562-5624**

You need to find a parent...   **206-586-2679**

You need to talk to someone...   **360-491-5715**

Child Support

Revenue Division
Dept. of Social & Health
Services
P.O. Box 9162
Olympia, WA 98507
206-459-6481

Domestic Violence

Washington State Coalition
Against Domestic Violence
8645 Martin Way NE
Suite 103
Lacey, WA 98516
360-407-0756

Washington Coalition of Sexual
Assault Programs
110 East Fifth Avenue
Suite 214
Olympia, WA 98501
360-754-7583

State Police

Washington State Police
P.O. Box 2527
Olympia, WA 98504

State Bar

Washington State Bar
Association
500 Westin Bldg.
2001 6th Ave.
Seattle, WA 98121
206-727-8200

West Virginia

Your child is missing... **800-843-5678**

Your child is being hurt... **800-352-6513**

You need to find a parent... **304-558-0461**

You need to talk to someone... **304-342-0497**

Child Support

Child Advocate Office
Dept. of Human Services
State Capitol Complex
Building 6, Room 812
Charleston, WV 25305
304-348-3780

Domestic Violence

West Virginia Coalition Against
Domestic Violence
181B Main Street
Sutton, WV 26601
304-765-2250

West Virginia Foundation for
Rape Information & Services
112 Braddock Street
Fairmont, WV 26554
304-366-9500

State Police

West Virginia State Police
725 Jefferson Rd.
South Charleston, WV 25309

State Bar

West Virginia Bar Association
100 Capitol Street
Charleston, WV 25301
304-342-1474

West Virginia State Bar
2006 Kanawha Blvd. E.
Charleston, WV 25311
304-558-2456

Wisconsin

Your child is missing...	**608-266-7314**
Your child is being hurt...	**800-422-4453**
You need to find a parent...	**608-267-4872**
You need to talk to someone...	**608-268-6000**

Child Support

Division of Economic Support
Bureau of Child Support
1 West Wilson Street
Madison, WI 53707
608-266-1175

Domestic Violence

Wisconsin Coalition Against
Domestic Violence
1400 East Washington Ave.
Suite 232
Madison, WI 53703
608-255-0539

Wisconsin Coalition Against
Sexual Assault
123 E. Main Street
2nd Floor
Madison, WI 53703
608-257-1516

State Police

Wisconsin Law Enforcement
Bureau
P.O. Box 2718
Madison, WI 53701

State Bar

State Bar of Wisconsin
402 W. Wilson
Madison, WI 53703
608-257-3838

Wyoming

Your child is missing...   **307-777-7537**

Your child is being hurt...   **800-422-4453**

You need to find a parent...   **307-777-6067**

You need to talk to someone... **307-362-3333**

Child Support

Child Support Enforcement
Dept. of Health & Social
Services
Hathaway Building
Cheyenne, WY 82002
307-777-7892

Domestic Violence

Wyoming Coalition Against
Domestic Violence and Sexual
Assault
P.O. Box 236
Laramie, WY 82073

State Police

Wyoming Criminal Investigation
Bureau
316 W. 22nd St.
Cheyenne, WY 85002

State Bar

Wyoming State Bar
500 Randall Avenue
Cheyenne, WY 82001
307-632-9061

WINNER!

Benjamin Franklin Award
Writer's Digest Magazine
National Competition

Child Custody Made Simple is an indispensable guide to the strange, sometimes bewildering world of family courts. Written in clear, simple language, it answers many questions posed by separated, divorced, or never-married parents. Packed with expert tips, this book shows how to succeed in the brave new world of single parenting.

096494040X, 480 pages, $21.95

"*Child Custody Made Simple* is an excellent starting point. Each chapter is chock full of both basic information and detailed examples that walk you through the child custody process."
—David Levy, President, Children's Rights Council

"The power of this book rests in Watnik's understanding of the complex negotiations that drive child custody... an excellent book." —Margorie L. Engel, Author, The Divorce Decisions Workbook

"*Child Custody Made Simple* offers a detailed chronology of what happens during a divorce. I recommend it."
—Andrea Engber, National Organization of Single Mothers

"This comprehensive legal guide to child custody... is a must-read for the uninitiated. I highly recommend it."
—Ralph Warner, Publisher, Nolo Press

Single Parent Press

Name

Address

City   State   Zip

Phone / Fax   Email

I Would Like to Order

Qty	Item	Price	Size	Total
	Divorce First Aid	$12.95		
	Child Custody Made Simple	$21.95		
	Subtotal			
	Tax (CA add 8.25%)			
	Shipping			
	TOTAL			

Payment Method

☐ Check   ☐ Visa   ☐ MasterCard   ☐ American Express

Card Number   Expiration Date

Signature

Make checks payable to *Single Parent Press.* Please do not send cash.

Shipping   ## To Order

$4.00   One item   Phone   (909) 624-6058
+$1.00 Each additional item Fax   (909) 624-2208

Single Parent Press, P.O. Box 1298, Claremont, CA 91711